CHARLES DICKENS:
DAVID COPPERFIELD

by

Philip Collins
Professor of English
University of Leicester

EDWARD ARNOLD

823.09
DIC

First published 1977 by
Edward Arnold (Publishers) Ltd
25 Hill Street, London W1X 8LL

Cloth edition ISBN: 0 7131 5935 9
Paper edition ISBN: 0 7131 5936 7

By the same author:
James Boswell (1956)
Dickens and Crime (1962)
Dickens and Education (1963)
The Impress of the Moving Age (1965)
(ed.) *Dickens: The Critical Heritage* (1971)
Dickens: Bleak House (1971)
Reading Aloud: A Victorian Métier (1972)
(ed.) *Charles Dickens: The Public Readings* (1975)

Printed in Great Britain by
The Camelot Press Ltd, Southampton

16,098

STUDIES IN ENGLISH LITERATURE No. 67

General Editor

David Daiches

Professor of English in the University of Sussex

Already published in the series:

Already published in the series *(continued)*:

Dedication

The author dedicates this booklet to his younger son Marcus, who likes Clara Peggotty and Mr Dick best, and hates Miss Murdstone because she says 'Generally speaking, I don't like boys.'

General Preface

The object of this series is to provide studies of individual novels, plays and groups of poems and essays which are known to be widely read by students. The emphasis is on classification and evaluation; biographical and historical facts, while they may be discussed when they throw light on particular elements in a writer's work, are generally subordinated to critical discussion. What kind of work is this? What exactly goes on here? How good is this work, and why? These are the questions that each writer will try to answer.

It should be emphasized that these studies are written on the assumption that the reader has already read carefully the work discussed. The objective is not to enable students to deliver opinions about works they have not read, nor is it to provide ready-made ideas to be applied to works that have been read. In one sense all critical interpretation can be regarded as foisting opinions on readers, but to accept this is to deny the advantages of any sort of critical discussion directed at students or indeed at anybody else. The aim of these studies is to provide what Coleridge called in another context 'aids to reflection' about the works discussed. The interpretations are offered as suggestive rather than as definitive, in the hope of stimulating the reader into developing further his own insights. This is after all the function of all critical discourse among sensible people.

Because of the interest which this kind of study has aroused, it has been decided to extend it first from merely English literature to include also some selected works of American literature and now further to include selected works in English by Commonwealth writers. The criterion will remain that the book studied is important in itself and is widely read by students.

DAVID DAICHES

Contents

Acknowledgements

The Publishers' thanks are due to Penguin Books Ltd for permission to reproduce copyright material from Charles Dickens: *David Copperfield*, edited by Trevor Blount (Penguin English Library 1966), © Trevor Blount 1966

1. The Author, the Hero and the Narratives

'I have just finished *Copperfield* and don't know whether to laugh or cry,' Dickens wrote to his friend Angela Burdett Coutts on 23 October 1850 (*N* II, 241.[1] Two days earlier, when within three pages of the end, he had written to another intimate friend (John Forster, his future biographer): 'Oh, my dear Forster, if I were to say half of what *Copperfield* makes me feel to-night, how strangely, even to you, I should be turned inside out! I seem to be sending part of myself into the Shadowy World' (*Life*, 547). Several points emerge here, to all of which we shall return. First, note the date: the novel was being written, as well as published, serially, and the final instalment (a double number) was on sale at the end of October, only a week after Dickens had finished writing it. He had rarely been as much as a fortnight ahead of the monthly publication date. Secondly, his not knowing whether to laugh or cry refers not only to the mixed feelings with which he completed any such large task but also to the novel's own emotional mixture. In Micawber it has one of the great comic characters of English literature, and there is much other comedy besides. It is a story with a happy ending, too: 'I had advanced in fame and fortune, my domestic joy was perfect, I had been married ten happy years . . . (63: 939).[2] But the story also contains both such obviously pathetic episodes as the deaths of David's mother and of Dora, and an element of suffering and sadness, too, of which Dickens

---

[1] References to frequently-cited books will be given in the text. *N=The Letters of Charles Dickens*, ed. Walter Dexter (3 vols, London 1938), the Nonesuch Edition. *Life*=Forster's *Life of Charles Dickens*, ed. J. W. T. Ley (London 1928). *DCH=Dickens: the Critical Heritage*, ed. Philip Collins (London 1971).

[2] Quotations from the novel are taken from the Penguin English Library reprint, ed. Trevor Blount (1966). References cite chapter and, after the colon, page-number.

himself was very conscious. As he wrote in 1855 during a period of despondency:

> Why is it, that as with poor David, a sense comes always crushing on me now, when I fall into low spirits, as of one happiness I have missed in life, and one friend and companion I have never made? (*Life*, 639)

A third feature of my opening quotations is Dickens's strong sense of identification with the book and its hero. The phrase about 'sending part of myself into the Shadowy World' recurs of course in the 1850 Preface, which is uncommonly emotional for him ('in danger of wearying the reader whom I love, with personal confidences, and private emotions'). In a later Preface (1869) he told his readers, as he had meanwhile told many friends, that this was his 'favourite child': 'Of all my books, I like this the best.' (The public reading from *Copperfield* which he devised in 1861 was his favourite reading, too.) As Forster's *Life* (1872–4) disclosed in detail, there were indeed substantial overlaps between David and his creator: even members of Dickens's family were startled to discover their extent. But readers had always suspected that some such relationship existed. When Dickens was to meet Queen Victoria in 1870, she was briefed in advance: 'it is supposed that [*David Copperfield*] gives or at least gives a hint of the narrative of the author's early life.' As another contemporary put it, perhaps with some exaggeration, 'the public settled, without hesitation, that "David Copperfield" is another name for Charles Dickens' (*Daily News*, 1 March 1852). David's having become a popular novelist, and telling the story himself, were among the obvious encouragements for them to make this identification, and the Preface did not discourage such speculation. How useful, or distracting, or irrelevant it now is for readers to see David as some kind of projection of Dickens must be discussed further. Dickens, an author acutely aware of his public, must (it may reasonably be guessed) have realized that they were likely to jump to the conclusion that he was unusually close to the hero of this novel: and this realization doubtless affected his handling of character and narrative. Subtler pressures, too, of which he might be incompletely aware, affected him, as they must affect any author who incorporates into a fiction substantial amounts of his own personality, experiences and intimate relationships with parents, spouse and suchlike.

How his public would take a novel which they might suspect was about himself set Dickens trickier problems of tact than, two years earlier, Charlotte Brontë had faced, as the author of a first novel, *Jane*

Eyre: an Autobiography. Edited by Currer Bell (1847). She wrote in the first person, and readers rightly detected a note of autobiographical truth behind the narrative: but she was unknown, and writing pseudonymously. In 1849–50, when *Copperfield* was serialized, Dickens had been a popular novelist for fourteen years (just about as long as David has been a novelist at the end of his narrative): he was very well known, and many readers knew some basic facts about his life and career, such as his having been, like David, a reporter in Parliament. And this was the first time he had written a first-person novel. His doing so had begun from a desire to experiment, not a desire to write about himself. Late in 1848, Forster recalls, 'Dickens's thoughts were turning much to the form his next book should assume. A suggestion that he should write it in the first person, by way of a change, had been thrown out by me, which he took at once very gravely . . . though as yet not dreaming of any public use of his early personal trials' (*Life*, 522–3). Forster's advice may have been prompted by the great recent success of *Jane Eyre*, or maybe by his having read, about that time, part of the autobiographical manuscript which Dickens had started writing, and then abandoned, sometime around 1845–8. Certainly it is interesting that, by Forster's account, *Copperfield* began, not from a theme or situation or autobiographical impulse, but from a technical adventurousness about what 'form his next book should assume.'[3]

Appropriately to its first-person form, the novel was concerned much more, and more intimately, with its hero than Dickens's previous novels had been. This was signalled in the full title (not given in many reprints)—*The Personal History, Adventures, Experience and Observation of David Copperfield the Younger, of Blunderstone Rookery. (Which He never meant to be Published on any Account).* Even the shorter title, which appears

[3] A somewhat different and probably less reliable account of the novel's origins is given by Dickens's son Charley, in his Introduction to the 1892 Macmillan reprint. His mother, he wrote, particularly wanted him to make it known that (despite what Forster had recorded in the *Life*) she did know of the autobiographical fragment: Dickens had read it to her and expressed his intention of publishing it. She tried to dissuade him 'on the ground that he had spoken with undue harshness of his father, and, especially, of his mother: and with so much success that he eventually decided that he would be satisfied with working it into *David Copperfield*, and would give up the idea of publishing it as it stood.' Dickens, it should be added, had once before begun a major attempt at first-person narration: the opening of *The Old Curiosity Shop* is ostensibly told by 'an old man', but at the end of chapter 3 Dickens briskly jettisons this narrator and tells the story in his usual fashion.

on the first page, and which Dickens uses in all his monthly memoranda ('Number-Plans'), is *[The] Personal History and Experience of David Copperfied [the Younger]*—and this too contrasts with the formula which he had used for the full titles of *Nickleby* and *Chuzzlewit*, which had begun with the more conventional and external *The Life and Adventures of.* . . . Some further indications of Dickens's intentions, as he embarked upon the novel, may be gained from earlier and rejected titles and surnames. Two months before the first instalment appeared, the title was *Mag's Diversions. Being the personal history of Mr Thomas Mag the Younger, of Blunderstone House.* Dickens was evidently intrigued by the 'blunder' notion which he had lately (on 9 January 1849) found, by happy chance, given a local habitation on a signpost which he passed as he walked along the road from Lowestoft to Yarmouth 'while I was meditating the story, and chose Blunderstone for the sound of its name' (*N* II, 194, 484). He had not actually visited the village of Blunderston—as it is correctly spelt—but its name chimed with the implications of the hero's surname at that time, Mag. The point was to have been made clear by a motto: 'And in short it led to the very Mag's Diversions. *Old Saying.*' This old saying meant a shambles, a cock-up, a mess. Obviously the hero was to make some bad mistakes, or suffer considerable misfortune. Other surnames contemplated for the hero were Wellbury, Flowerbury, Magbury, Trotfield, Trotbury, Spankle, Copperboy, Topflower, Copperstone. Here one notes the recurrence of *field/flower* elements (compare David's nicknames 'Young Innocence' and 'Daisy'), and of *bury* and *stone* (the novel is to be much concerned with deaths and with the past). In these preliminary notes, Thomas Mag was sometimes re-christened David; more significantly, David Copperfield is twice renamed 'Charles'.

It was, Forster recalled, his completing the second chapter that 'defined to himself, more clearly than before, the character of the book'—whereupon he rejected the title which he then favoured (*The Copperfield Survey of the World as it Rolled*) for one more strictly personal. This second chapter, 'I Observe', had given him his first experience of true first-person narration in a novel of 'Retrospect' (a term which occurs in four chapter-titles). Chapter 1, 'I am Born', is basically an omniscient-narrator piece, told in the first person; David had not 'observed' the events leading up to his birth, and Dickens avails himself of the literary convention whereby narrators of first-person novels are endowed with the ability to write dialogues which they did not hear and provide scene-setting which no one is likely to have reported to them (for instance, the paragraph about the wind in the elms, which 'bent to one another, like giants who were whispering secrets' (1: 53–4)). But with 'The first objects that assume a distinct presence before me, as I look far back . . .' (the opening words of chapter 2) the novel assumes its true form. As David later says, 'this narrative is my written memory' (58: 889), and this is a novel of memory not only in the obvious sense that it is David's retrospective account of what he has been and experienced and observed, but also in that it explores the nature, functioning and value of memory. Thus, chapter 2 continues with a searching and discrimination among memories: 'I believe I can remember. . . . I have an impression on my mind which I cannot distinguish from actual remembrance. . . . This may be fancy, though. . . . What else do I remember? Let me see. . . .' (2: 61)—and, as will be shown, that 'see' is often taken very literally, with phrases such as 'At this minute I see him' (2: 68) or 'I see it now' (5: 129) recurring, followed by vividly particularized descriptions. Moreover, those opening paragraphs of chapter 2 start up the important topic of the pleasures and benefits of memory—of how, specifically, in this story of a boy's growth into manhood, 'The Child is father of the Man', and how the man in living touch with his own childhood (another Wordsworthian theme) is the better for it:

> I think the memory of most of us can go further back into such times than many of us suppose; just as I believe the power of observation in numbers of very young children to be quite wonderful for its closeness and accuracy. Indeed, I think that most grown men who are remarkable in this respect, may with greater propriety be said not to have lost the faculty, than to have acquired it; the rather, as I generally observe such men to retain a certain freshness, and gentleness, and capacity of being pleased, which are also an inheritance they have preserved from their childhood. (2: 61)

Behind this one hears Wordsworth's 'That in this moment there is life and food / For future years', his being 'well pleased to recognize' in the memory of his perceptions

> The anchor of my purest thoughts, the nurse,
> The guide, the guardian of my heart, and soul
> Of all my moral being.[4]

---

[4] 'Lines composed a few miles above Tintern Abbey', ll. 65–6, 108–12. For Dickens's congruence with this aspect of Romanticism, cf. also S. T. Coleridge, in

Much later in the narrative, David tells us that he became a successful novelist—not of course with his lifestory ('this manuscript is intended for no eyes but mine' (42: 671))—but the only information given about his novels is that they too are largely exercises in memory, or semi-autobiographical—a species of writing for which David had long been in training. Recall the end of the Murdstone and Grinby chapter:

> I fitted my old books to my altered life, and made stories for myself, out of the streets, and out of men and women. . . . When my thoughts go back, now, to that slow agony of my youth, I wonder how much of the histories I invented for such people hangs like a mist of fancy over well-remembered facts! [Another pertinent 'wondering' here, one might interject, about how the memory operates—about how 'well-remembered facts' become embroidered, modified, transformed, when viewed through 'a mist of fancy' not peculiar to novelists.] When I tread the old ground, I do not wonder that I seem to see and pity, going on before me, an innocent romantic boy, making his imaginative world out of such strange experiences and sordid things!
>
> (11: 224-5)

Accordingly, when he is writing his first novel, David's thoughts are busy with 'childish recollections and later fancies, the ghosts of half-formed hopes, the broken shadows of disappointments dimly seen and understood, the blending of imagination and experience' (46: 734), and his second novel is 'a Story, with a purpose growing, not remotely, out of my experience' (58: 889)—terms which strongly suggest the relationship between Dickens and *David Copperfield*.

For Dickens's novel is eminently a 'blending of imagination and experience': or, as he put it after writing one of the most closely autobiographical passages (the Murdstone and Grinby episode in chapter 11, much of it copied verbatim from his fragmentary manuscript autobiography), 'I really think I have done it ingeniously, and with a

---

The Friend: 'To carry on the feelings of childhood into the powers of manhood, to combine the child's sense of wonder and novelty with the appearances which every day for perhaps forty years have rendered familiar, . . . this is the character and privilege of genius.' Dickens democratizes the notion, granting Coleridge's 'privilege of genius' to 'most of us . . . numbers of very young children' (2: 61, quoted above). A Dickens essay of this period is very germane to this topic: 'Where we stopped growing', *Household Words*, 1 January 1853, reprinted in *Miscellaneous Papers*, ed. B. W. Matz (London 1908).

very complicated interweaving of truth and fiction' (*Life*, 497).
Ingeniously, indeed: and it is far from true (as some have argued) that
Copperfield is so much Dickens's autobiography that when he introduces
fictitious elements his powers are likely to desert him. The novel has
splendid successes, and flaws, both in the parts which derive most closely
from personal experience, and in those which are, apparently, wholly the
product of imagination. But it is a 'blending' in other respects, too: a
mixture, as has been noted, of tears and laughter (early-Victorian readers
greatly relished this combination). For to some extent it pursues the aims
which Dickens had proclaimed for *Pickwick* and *Nickleby*: 'to amuse, by
producing a rapid succession of characters and incidents, and describing
them as cheerfully and pleasantly as in us lies; . . . to enlist both [our
readers'] heartiest merriment, and their kindliest sympathies.' A mixture
also, and again much to the taste of the time and very agreeable to
Dickens's genius, of many other narrative and emotional elements:
comedy and pathos, but love and sentiment, too, and mystery, villainy,
exciting event, social satire, political commentary. Dickens's art, like
Shakespeare's, is always inclusive: a big cast, a lot happening, a bit of
everything. *David Copperfield* differs, though, from the novels written just
before and after it, in that it is less concerned with 'the Condition of
England question', with social values and political institutions. Also it
contains no murder or violent crime, such as occur in most Dickens
novels, though the deathrate remains high (eight characters die) and,
instead of the usual penultimate flight-and-pursuit episode, *Copperfield*
has the violent climactic event of the Storm, in which two characters
meet a sudden death. All this suggests another mixture, which I want
now to discuss further—the 'blending' of a study of David's personal
development ('the story of his life from year to year', to adapt one of
Dickens's favourite Shakespearian allusions) with the well-populated
multi-plot narrative dear to Dickens and his readers.

The novel, I have said, is more deeply and continuously concerned
with its hero's personality and development than its predecessors had
been. In starting with his birth and childhood, Dickens was continuing a
tradition which he had already greatly amplified in *Oliver Twist* (1837–9)
and *Dombey and Son* (1846–8) which also begin with a birth in chapter 1:
and he had given much attention to childhood in his presentations of
Dotheboys Hall, and of such characters as Barnaby Rudge, Little Nell
and Tiny Tim. But Oliver is still a boy at the end of his novel, and Paul
Dombey dies in childhood, early in the story. Never before had Dickens

taken a character from birth to maturity. He only did so once again, in
Great Expectations (1860–1); and Pip offers fascinating parallels to, and
differences from, David. David's childhood is very troubled, and, though
the novel ends with the conventional sound of happy wedding-bells, he
has, unusually in fiction of that period, been married already, his first
marriage having resulted (in the often-quoted words) from 'the first
mistaken impulse of an undisciplined heart'. So Dickens has plenty of
matter here—and David also has to earn his living, and to make his way
in the world, again with several false starts. In these aspects, then, the
novel is a *Bildungsroman* (concerned with its hero's development, his
'apprenticeship to life'—the familiar theme of a young person's 'entrance
into the world'). Also, since its hero becomes a novelist, it is, to an extent
which I shall discuss later, a 'Portrait of an Artist as a Young Man'—a
'Portrait of *the* Artist' if David's closeness to Dickens is taken into
account.[5] While Copperfield was being serialized, Wordsworth's *Prelude*
was published posthumously, and commentators have remarked on the
affinities, and possible relationship, between these two works.
Wordsworth had entitled his poem 'The Growth of a Poet's Mind':
might *Copperfield* have been subtitled 'The Growth of a Novelist's
Mind'? Another great confessional work appeared in the same year, 1850:
Tennyson's *In Memoriam*, originally entitled 'The Way of a Soul'. David,
it will be suggested below, has no 'soul', in Tennyson's sense, to be saved
or lost or disturbed, but the two works present some analogies.[6]

How *David Copperfield* enlarges upon the basic form of the
Bildungsroman may be suggested by a comparison—to which I shall
return—with that other semi-autobiographical novel published two
years earlier, *Jane Eyre*. 'I have read *David Copperfield*,' Charlotte Brontë

[5] On *David Copperfield*, in relation to these forms, see the relevant chapters of
Jerome Hamilton Buckley, *Season of Youth: the Bildungsroman from Dickens to
Golding* (Cambridge, Mass. 1974), and Maurice Beebe, *Ivory Towers and Sacred
Founts: the Artist as Hero in Fiction* (New York 1964).

[6] A closer analogy exists between *Copperfield* and Tennyson's *Maud* (1855):
both favourite works of their authors, both with heroes akin to them and with
whom they were prone to identify themselves, and both with heroines, too, based
upon women in their lives. Both purport to show the dangers, and the eventual
overcoming, of an 'undisciplined heart' (Tennyson calls it 'mismanaged
imagination'). Critics have generally felt less satisfied, in both works, by the
'solution' than by the earlier stages of the hero's predicament. The hero of *Maud*
does not marry an Agnes, but arguably Tennyson himself did. See Ralph Rader's
Tennyson's Maud: the Biographical Genesis (Berkeley 1963), a reading of which
suggested this comparison, though Rader does not make it.

wrote to her publisher, while it was being serialized; 'it seems to me very good—admirable in parts. You said it had an affinity with *Jane Eyre*. It has, now and then—only what an advantage has Dickens in his varied knowledge of men and things!'[7] The advantages do not all lie with Dickens; partly because he takes in so much else, we do not, I think, know David as intensely or in such complexity as we know Jane. But Dickens's 'varied knowledge of men and things' is put to good service. The *Copperfield Survey of the World as it Rolled*—to revert to that rejected but not inappropriate title—includes incomparably more incident, and a much great number and variety of characters, than *Jane Eyre*, the world of which is, by comparison, sparsely populated despite Jane's various changes of scene. Only a handful of characters in *Jane Eyre* have much imaginative potency; in *David Copperfield*, even such bit-players as Mr Chillip or Mrs Crupp or Julia Mills or Dora's aunts remain vivid in the memory, and there are many such. To confine attention, for the moment, to those parts of the novel in which David is most fully involved: his life, as was noted, is disturbed and eventful, particularly in its earlier phases. Soon bereft of parents, and with no brothers or sisters, he quickly moves through a series of environments, major characters from which are apt to return into the narrative at some later stage, often by coincidence. Dickens was fond of this variant on the picaresque tradition: Nicholas Nickleby and his sister, for instance, had between them got, or nearly got, eight jobs, which encounters had introduced many environments and groups of characters.

Thus, David starts at Blunderstone; Peggotty of course survives from that part of his life as an important character, but also Miss Murdstone reappears as Dora Spenlow's protectress ('I don't think I was much astonished,' David remarks [26: 450], nor are we), and with like inevitability Mr Murdstone, needing the services of Doctors' Commons, consults David's firm (ch. 33). Clara Peggotty takes David to Yarmouth, and he remains caught up with that group in many later chapters, not only as an affectionate friend who revisits them but also because, by

[7] Letter to W. S. Williams, 13 September 1849. *Copperfield*, many critics have argued, was influenced by *Jane Eyre*: some early episodes are similar, and they are narrated in the first-person and have a *Bildungsroman* structure. But in a recently-discovered and apparently authentic account of his conversation, Dickens is recorded as saying (years after *Copperfield*) that he 'had not read *Jane Eyre* and said he never would as he disapproved of the whole [Brontë] school' (*Dickensian* LXXI (1975), 5).

introducing Steerforth, he unwittingly brings sorrow and disgrace upon them; in chapter 55, by multiple coincidence, David is at Yarmouth when Steerforth's ship, having come all the way from Spain, sinks there, and Ham, unaware of whom he is trying to save, drowns with his former rival. David's next new environment, after Yarmouth, is Salem House: here he meets Steerforth and Traddles, both of whom he is to run into again later, with many consequences for the plotting and the pattern of the story—and Creakle too is granted a late re-entry (in chapter 61), irrelevant and implausible though it is. Of the Murdstone and Grinby episode which follows nothing remains except the deeply painful memory—and of course the Micawbers, with whom David lodges at that time, and who 'turn up' in several coincidental ways later. He then escapes to Kent, thus meeting Betsey and Mr Dick, the Wickfields and the Heeps and the Strongs. By now, some subsidiary actions are beginning to emerge, which will impinge upon David's fate or self-understanding. In chapter 15, he has met at Mr Wickfield's the destined heroine, his union with whom will conclude the book, and the tone in which she is introduced signals this clearly: 'I never have forgotten',—'I never shall forget', etc. (15: 279)—though Dickens's manuscript jotting for chapter 15, 'Introduction of the real heroine', indicates that a mistaken heroine or so are to intervene. How the Agnes story will develop is suggested by her father's weakness for the bottle and Uriah Heep's evident villainy. Dickens emphasizes this by ending chapter 15 (and Number 5) on the odiousness of Uriah, who thus immediately represents a twofold threat to Agnes. He will, it is obvious, try both to possess her sexually and to seize her family's fortune. Then, in chapter 16, Jack Maldon leaves for India brandishing a cherry-coloured ribbon, and Annie Strong swoons. Manifestly, a sub-plot is implicit here.

With David's calf-love for Miss Shepherd and the eldest Miss Larkins (ch. 18), he reaches adolescence, and the theme of his love-life begins, which is to prove a much more prominent topic than the other features of his 'entrance into the world' (his jobs, for instance). His inflammability—never extraordinary nor more reprehensible than most men's errors at that age—had of course been indicated much earlier in his childhood adoration of Little Emily. Miss Larkins is a brief and superficial experience of the 'mistaken impulse of an undisciplined heart'; Dora will be a more permanent and serious one. By now the story is less than a third told, but most of the major characters and plot-lines (except for the Spenlows) have been introduced, and already an important figure from an earlier phase has re-entered, by coincidence. In chapter 17 ('Somebody Turns Up'), David is having tea with the Heeps—an episode in which every touch is both diverting and exquisitely excruciating, and one which nicely displays an important respect in which David is far from being like Dickens (his Daisy-like innocence, his complete inability here to cope with the Heeps)—and he looks longingly towards the door:

I had begun to be a little uncomfortable, and to wish myself well out of the visit, when a figure coming down the street passed the door—it stood open to air the room, which was warm, the weather being close for the time of year—came back again, looked in, and walked in, exclaiming loudly, 'Copperfield! Is is possible?'

It was Mr Micawber! It was Mr Micawber, with his eye-glass, and his walking-stick, and his shirt-collar, and his genteel air, and the condescending roll in his voice, all complete!

'My dear Copperfield,' said Mr Micawber, putting out his hand, 'this is indeed a meeting which is calculated to impress the mind with a sense of the instability and uncertainty of all human—in short, it is a most extraordinary meeting. . . .'

I cannot say—I really can*not* say—that I was glad to see Mr Micawber there; but I was glad to see him too, and shook hands with him, heartily, inquiring how Mrs Micawber was.   (17: 314–15)

If David is embarrassed to see Micawber just there and then, the reader is delighted: and it is typical of Dickens's art to use coincidence so ruthlessly (and so openly—'Is it possible?') to restore a notable character or to keep the plot running. Dickens, it should be added, was by no means alone among the novelists of his period in using coincidence so liberally: recall Jane Eyre's collapsing unawares on her long-lost relatives' doorstep, or the chances which affect the plots of George Eliot, a novelist much more committed to 'realism' than Dickens.[8]

Micawber, having turned up in chapter 17, disappears again until chapter 27. David had run into Traddles in chapter 25, and now 'perhaps, for no better reason than because there was a certain similarity in the sound of [Mrs Crupp's] word skittles and Traddles' (what a contrivance!) he looks him up. 'The general air of [his street] reminded

[8] This technique is intelligently discussed by David Goldknopf in his *The Life of the Novel* (Chicago 1972), chapter 9, 'What coincidence means in the Victorian novel'.

me forcibly of the days when I lived with Mr and Mrs Micawber'—and no reader will be surprised, despite David's exclamation marks, when a few pages later it transpires that Micawber is Traddles's landlord, nor that when he walks in he is 'not a bit changed—his tights, his stick, his shirt-collar, and his eye-glass, all the same as ever' (27: 461, 467)—'Mr Micawber, . . . all complete', as he was at his previous re-entry, and always is. So David invites Traddles and the Micawbers to dinner (ch. 28), when, undaunted by their failure in the Medway coal-trade and in corn ('For corn . . . may be gentlemanly, but it is not remunerative. Commission to the extent of two and ninepence in a fortnight cannot, however limited our ideas, be considered remunerative' [28: 478]), they contemplate the prospects of banking and of, more simply, 'throwing down the gauntlet to society' and saying, in effect, 'Show me who will take that up. Let the party immediately step forward' (28: 480). They next appear in chapter 36, when they are, very conveniently, going off to one of the provincial outposts of the story, Uriah Heep having been the party to step forward and take up the Micawber gauntlet. This strains belief more than the coincidences do: Uriah would never employ an old ally of David's, and could hardly fancy that Micawber would prove an effective confidential secretary for his nefarious purposes; nor is Micawber's exultation in being re-united with Uriah as credible as, say, his vision of himself upon the Woolsack. More improbable still is his having the persistence and resourcefulness, even with Traddles's backing, to collect and marshal a watertight case against Uriah. We acquiesce because of the sheer joy and the moral justice of it, but this is more implausible than the oft-cited improbability of his making good in Australia, one of those convenient colonies to which Victorian novelists were fond of 'exporting their surplus population' (to quote the great emigration slogan of the day, for emigration was then a notable feature of British life, as well as of British fiction; only two of Dickens's seven sons, for instance, made their careers at home).

I have run ahead along the Micawber line, leaving David and the other actions at chapter 18, to illustrate one feature about how the novel works: the recurrence of characters from earlier phases of the action, often coincidentally thrown into new groupings. Thus, as we have seen, Micawber, first encountered in the Murdstone and Grinby period, reappears successively in conjunction with the Heeps, with Traddles, and with the firm of Wickfield and Heep, before he emigrates with the Peggotty group and discovers that his most distinguished fellow-citizen in Port Middlebay is Dr Mell (given a brief re-entry 56 chapters after his last appearance). Even the curiously intrusive prison episode (ch. 61), besides serving its main function—irrelevant to the novel, for it is a journalistic lampoon of a recent experiment in penology—enables Dickens not only to give a final kick to Creakle and a bouquet to Miss Mowcher, but also to dispose finally of survivors from two sub-plots, Uriah Heep and Steerforth's factotum Littimer. Dickens's fictional world is populous but tidy—a world with abundant poetic justice, problems solved, and no loose ends. The completeness of the ending, which accounts appropriately for Julia Mills, the Micawber children and Traddles's sisters-in-law, comes from a Dickens fundamentally confident that he inhabits a rational universe where things work out right. David expresses due satisfaction over Peggotty's arrival with news from Australia: without it, 'one thread in the web I have spun would have a ravelled end' (63: 939).

To return to chapter 18 ('A Retrospect'): this ends David's childhood and schooldays, with one of his rare but credibilizing confessions that he does not remember anything much about what should have been a crucial event, his leaving school:

> I try in vain to recall how I felt about it, and what its circumstances were; but it is not momentous in my recollection. I suppose the opening prospect confused me. I know that my juvenile experiences went for little or nothing then; and that life was more like a great fairy story, which I was just about to begin to read, than anything else.
>
> (19: 330)

(That 'great fairy story' feeling, it may be remarked, is an instance of David's 'romantic and dreamy' nature, his 'wandering ardour and unsettled purpose' [7: 146, 35: 581], which are to lead him astray.) He has now completed his formal education, at his mother's knee and at two schools, and his not less important informal and affective education—the influence of his mother and of the large number of parental figures who have cared for or maltreated him, and the impact of the bottling warehouse and other formative experiences. Now, after a pause before Betsey settles him in a profession, he begins the world. He joins Doctors' Commons—occasion, later, for a little minor institutional criticism, but we never see David seriously at work there. Nor indeed does Dickens spend many words on David's later occupations, as Dr Strong's part-time secretary (manifestly Dr Strong has been moved to London, and employs

David, so that the Annie Strong plot can be kept going without continual forays to Canterbury), or as a parliamentary reporter or an author. As has been noted, it is David's personal, emotional and domestic life that monopolizes attention: but this of course is very general in novels.

As an indication of what kind of novelist Dickens is, it is worth remarking here on possibilities which he does *not* explore in this, his most elaborate and self-conscious hero so far. David suffers from no moral or spiritual or ideological perplexities. He makes mistakes, of course; he is 'blind, blind, blind' (35: 565) not only to the qualities of Dora and Agnes, and to his own needs, but also, and fatally for others, to Steerforth's weaknesses. But when, for instance, he at last acknowledges to himself that marrying Dora has proved a disappointment, he does so with little tension or struggle, let alone any temptation to end or mitigate this state of affairs by drastic or unconventional action. Instead, he resolves 'henceforth to be satisfied with my child-wife . . . I loved my wife dearly, and I was happy; but . . . there was always something wanting.' And a page later, he has his reward: 'But, as that year wore on, Dora was not strong' (48: 763, 765, 766). She appears only once more, and briefly, before her deathbed scene (ch. 53), and even at that stage David's emotions are not plumbed (how troubled, indeed, is he?). Chapter 54 begins: 'This is not the time at which I am to enter on the state of my mind beneath its load of sorrow' (54: 839). Why not? one objects: and when the time arrives (ch. 58), the grief and self-examination are limited, and are more concerned with his apparent loss of Agnes than with the tragedy of Dora's life and early death. Contrast with this the moral dilemmas into which Charlotte Brontë and George Eliot manoeuvre their fictional *alter egos*: should Jane Eyre sacrifice her principles by staying with the married Mr Rochester, or her selfhood by marrying St John Rivers? should Maggie Tulliver defy family prejudice by continuing to see Philip Wakem, and later should she, in a complex situation, marry or reject Stephen Guest? These are much tougher choices than any which David has to make. Similarly, David has no such uncertainties as were becoming a frequent topic in fiction at this time—the kind of question that Disraeli's heroes, for instance, find themselves asking: 'What is DUTY, and what is FAITH? What ought I to DO, and what ought I to BELIEVE?' (*Tancred* (1847), Bk. 2, ch. 1). 'Honest doubt' was a phrase of that day—it comes, of course, from *In Memoriam* (1850)—but David is never troubled about what Agnes is pointing upwards towards, nor about where his duty lies. Basil Willey made the point through a

THE AUTHOR, THE HERO AND THE NARRATIVES 21

comparison with *The Mill on the Floss* (1860): 'Am I made aware [in *Copperfield*] of a whole social and spiritual predicament as I am by George Eliot? . . . And had David a soul to be saved? It is significant that whereas he solaces himself with *Roderick Random* and *Humphry Clinker*, Maggie Tulliver reads Thomas à Kempis—and this experience changes her life' (*Listener*, 23 February 1950, 353). A final, and perhaps more surprising, example (given Dickens's reformist interests) is that David—unlike the heroes and heroines of so much contemporary fiction—settles without question, or any need to take his political bearings, into contemporary society, which in this novel, in contrast to the England of *Dombey and Son* before or *Bleak House* after it, is untroubled and untroubling—virtually unseen, indeed. Even in his professional life, David never feels much conscientious scruple about earning a livelihood out of 'that rotten old ecclesiastical cheese' (25: 425), Doctors' Commons. He uses some ironical phrases about this antique institution but, like his shrewd worldly wisdom about Mr Creakle's penological principles, these seem to be imposed upon him—to issue from Dickens rather than from the David we have known. Circumstances remove David from the Commons, and he does eventually make a moral gesture; when he is a prosperous author, he rejects offers of a percentage if he will allow unqualified nominees to practise in his name—'considering the Commons quite bad enough, without my doing anything to make it worse' (61: 918).

David is removed from the Commons partly because Dickens cannot allow so estimable a hero to spend a lifetime in such a dubious profession, but more because the hero needs to show strength of character, being tested by circumstances more exigent than that well-cushioned existence can provide. (Pip, in *Great Expectation*, gets the same salutary shock when Magwitch's fortune, like Betsey's, disappears.) David rises to the challenge immediately, with a good will, and effectively; he becomes 'such a determined character' (36: 590) that he surprises Traddles, and himself; he 'tames that savage stenographic mystery' and makes 'a respectable income by it' (43: 692); and in connection with this achievement, he announces his unexceptionable if unheroic and unexciting belief in what it is over-easy to depreciate as 'the bourgeois virtues':

    . . . the habits of punctuality, order, and diligence, . . . the determination to concentrate myself on one object at a time. . . . My meaning simply is, that whatever I have tried to do in life, I have tried with all my heart to do well; that whatever I have devoted myself to, I have devoted myself to completely; that, in great aims and in small, I have always been thoroughly in earnest . . . ; and there is no substitute for thorough-going, ardent, and sincere earnestness. Never to put one hand to anything, on which I could throw my whole self; and never to affect depreciation of my work, whatever it was; I find, now, to have been my golden rules. (42: 671)

Here, David is indistinguishable from his maker, and one may perhaps envy a society whose leading author and spokesman could, with such assurance and without embarrassment, enunciate convictions which have such a core of soundness. David's principles and intentions are always estimable; it is his judgment that goes awry. The two main plot-lines resulting from this deficiency start up as he enters manhood (ch. 19). He runs into Steerforth again, remains entirely under his spell despite the hints about his dangerous and depraved proclivities dropped by Rosa Dartle and later by Miss Mowcher, and introduces him to the Peggotty household (ch. 21). The conclusion of that chapter (and of Number 7) suggests clearly enough, to the reader though not at that stage to David, what will emerge from that encounter: '"A most engaging little Beauty!" said Steerforth. . . . "That's rather a chuckle-headed fellow for the girl; isn't he? . . . Daisy, I believe you are in earnest, and are good. I wish we all were!" . . .' (21: 376–7).

Soon afterwards, 'I Fall into Captivity' (the title of chapter 26): David meets Dora and loves her at first sight, and the main love-action is under way—for Dora survives until chapter 53, and Agnes comes into her own only in the final chapters. Agnes remains, however, an important presence throughout David's story, besides figuring in two of the main subplots, the Annie Strong one and the one involving her father, Uriah Heep and Micawber. Her significance for the hero is again signalled in chapter 25, rather misleadingly entitled 'Good and Bad Angels'. She of course is his good angel as well as his eventual reward, but Steerforth never really threatens to be David's bad angel. David's 'First Dissipation' (ch. 24) indeed takes place in Steerforth's company, but this is a mild affair of tiddliness and smoking cigars. David is never in danger of being corrupted by Steerforth into, for instance, regarding the Peggotty family as 'that sort of people' (20: 352), let alone into indulging in such profligacy as lurks behind Miss Mowcher's familiarities with Steerforth and is later manifested in his abduction of Emily. As the novelist and reviewer Mrs Oliphant remarked, in 1855,

(. . . it is the air and the breath of middle-class respectability which fills the books of Mr. Dickens. His heroes are not the young men of clubs and colleges. . . . They are spotless in their thoughts, their intentions, and wishes. Into those dens of vice, and unknown mysteries,) whither · · · the lordly Pelham [in Lytton's novel] may penetrate without harm, and which [Thackeray's] Messrs. Pendennis and Warrington frequent, that they may see 'life', David Copperfield could not enter without pollution. In the very heart and soul of him this young man is *respectable*. He is a great deal more; he is pure, a thoroughly refined and gentle-hearted boy; but his respectability is strong upon him.[9]

Steerforth is important as a foil to David, not an influence upon him—and as the protagonist of one of the main actions. Dickens, indeed, selected the Steerforth/Emily/Peggotty story, culminating in the Storm, as the narrative for his public reading from *Copperfield*, interspersing in it some episodes from David's courtship and Dora's housekeeping.

That mixture in the public reading (a ninety-minute abbreviation of these selected episodes) parallels the plan of the novel. As has been seen, like all of Dickens's other full-length novels, it contains several actions, linked because of the many connections between participants in them, and, in this first-person novel, further linked by David's being present, as agent or reporter, at the crucial or climactic episodes, at least, of them all. (Thus, 'I assist at an Explosion' [ch. 52]: he witnesses the unmasking of Uriah Heep, as, in chapter 45, he had duly been present at the *éclaircissement* between Annie Strong and her husband, though he had not been involved in either of these developments except as an occasional and troubled spectator. Hence, too, his opportune visit to Yarmouth in chapter 55, 'The Tempest'.) There are some other minor actions, too,

[9] *DCH*, 327–8. One comparison made here—between David and Pendennis—was a commonplace (see *DCH*, pp. 242–66). By coincidence, Thackeray was serializing his semi-autobiographical *Pendennis* (December 1848 to December 1850) just when *Copperfield* was appearing, and inevitably the two novels were widely reviewed together. Pen, like David, becomes a novelist, and Thackeray was much more candid than Dickens in identifying himself with his hero (he often referred to himself as 'Pen'). Lacking a father, like David and Steerforth, Pen is also the victim of an 'undisciplined heart': but he gets much closer to moral turpitude than David ever does. See below, p. 40, for a further comparison: but many more comparisons can usefully be made.

which have not been mentioned, such as the marriages of Clara Peggotty and Tommy Traddles, or the strange man haunting Betsey Trotwood. So there are many events which are not of David's making, though they involve people in whom he is keenly interested: and there are many characters who are more fully elaborated than is necessary for the impact they make upon David's fortunes or consciousness (the Micawbers are an obvious instance). Later (in Chapter 4) I shall discuss the quality and interest of the plot-lines in which David is not a protagonist, and ask what relevance they have in the pattern of the novel, to what degree they illuminate its hero, implicitly or explicitly, and how far, by their number and prominence, they distract attention from the hero—as does happen, I have suggested, when the exploration of David's feelings after Dora's death is deferred for forty-odd pages, which are filled with the hilarity of Micawber's preparations for sailing, the subdued pathos of Betsey's husband's death, and the drama of the Storm.

'First chapter funny—Then on to Emily' ran Dickens's memorandum for Number 10—the funny chapter being 'Mr Micawber's Gauntlet' (the dinner at Mrs Crupp's) and the Emily event being her running away from home, with David's last meeting with Steerforth, and Barkis's death, intervening. As a serial novelist, Dickens had to seek this balance of appeal—from the comic to the grave or exciting—not only in the novel as a whole but also in every instalment.[10] His readers spent eighteen months following the narrative, so he had to ensure, also, that important characters or plot-developments or ideas did not get submerged for too many months: his Number-plans are full, therefore, of reminders such as 'Carry the thread of Agnes through it all' (No. 12) or 'To carry on the thread of Uriah, carefully, and not obtrusively' (No. 13) or 'Mrs Steerforth and Miss Dartle, Carry Steerforth through by means of them' (No. 15). How well he contrived to keep his various plots moving in echelon is

[10] Many reprints fail to indicate the serial divisions, but they are worth attending to. Notice particularly how Dickens closes his instalments; he gave careful thought to what event, 'picture', phrase or notion to emphasize thus, as is clear from his memoranda (the 'Number-plans', printed and discussed in John Butt and Kathleen Tillotson, Dickens at Work (London 1957)). The serial divisions were as follows, Numbers being given in roman, and chapters in arabic, figures: I, 1–3; II, 4–6; III, 7–9; IV, 10–12; V, 13–15; VI, 16–18; VII, 19–21; VIII, 22–4; IX, 25–7; X, 28–31; XI, 32–4; XII, 35–7; XIII, 38–40; XIV, 41–3; XV, 44–6; XVI, 47–50; XVII, 51–3; XVIII, 54–7; XIX–XX, double number, 58–64. Numbers, each containing two illustrations and costing one shilling, were published from May 1849 to November 1850.

shown by the fact that so many of them arrive at a crisis-point, and then later are solved, in contiguous chapters. Thus, half-way through the novel (chs. 31–6), most of the plots come to the boil. Emily elopes with Steerforth (ch. 31), David becomes engaged to Dora (ch. 33), Betsey's fortune disappears, so that David must earn his living the hard way (ch. 34), Uriah is riding high in the Wickfield firm and household (ch. 35), Dr Strong re-enters the story, Jack Maldon returns to England and renews his assault upon Annie (chs. 35–6), and Mr Micawber gets involved in the plot by going off to Canterbury to work for Uriah (ch. 36). Almost all of these important developments are concluded within half-a-dozen chapters, too (chs. 50–5). Emily is restored to Mr Peggotty (ch. 50), Uriah is unmasked by Micawber (ch. 52), David's marriage to Dora is ended by her death (ch. 53), Betsey's husband dies, she gets her money back, and is thus able to help the Micawbers to emigrate to Australia with the Peggotty group (ch. 54), but the two men in the Emily story who cannot be accommodated in the happy ending which is manifestly now looming up—Ham and Steerforth—die together in the storm (ch. 55). This is a splendidly skilful handling of the technicalities of the multi-plot novel: but, to revert to a moment which has already been criticized and will be referred to again, David's postponing (ch. 54) his self-scrutiny at what should be a dramatic and psychological climax—the premature death of his wife Dora—illustrates the disadvantages or temptations of this kind of novel. A big moment can be muffed, or avoided, because so many other actions, also moving towards a climax, are competing for attention at that point. Intensity may be sacrificed to amplitude and variety. Or, to put this concretely, if we get less of David here than fully satisfies us, we get such large compensating doses of the Micawbers and Uriah Heep and other compelling figures, and of the narratives in which they are involved, that it is only in retrospect that we may notice and resent some evasiveness in the presentation of David's emotional development: for the loss of a wife, and of their expected firstborn before that, should have meant a great deal more to a man than is here offered, unless the point about him be (as is certainly not implied here) that he is emotionally anaesthetized.

A serial novelist's basic strategy must, obviously, include inducements for the reader to buy the next instalment: and this was no bad discipline for a Victorian multi-plot storyteller, and was one reason why experienced serialists like Dickens developed a strong narrative thrust. These features of serialization help also to explain why *David Copperfield* has the 'blending', the variety, indicated above—for a final point about this form of serialization was that the novel had to be lengthy. Dickens was sticking here to the pattern he had invented and popularized in his first novel, *Pickwick Papers* (1836–7), twenty Numbers with 32 closely-printed pages each. And the variety in *David Copperfield* explains why some critics, such as G. K. Chesterton, who argue that Dickens failed badly with the adult David, have nevertheless regarded this as his best and strongest novel—as it has certainly always been one of the two or three most popular novels he ever wrote.

2. The Child Who is Father of the Man

Edmund Wilson, seeing *David Copperfield* in relation to Dickens's development ('It is a departure from the series of his social novels'), judges it to be 'not one of Dickens's deepest books: it is something in the nature of a holiday': but 'in the first half, at any rate, Dickens strikes an enchanting vein which he had never quite found before and which he was never to find again. It is the poem of an idealized version of the loves and fears and wonders of childhood.'[1] I shall return to that 'holiday' judgment, and to the reservation implicit in 'idealized': what now concerns me is the rendering of childhood experience and emotion, 'poetic' indeed in its density, immediacy and sensuousness.

Within a page, the 'I Observe' chapter invokes sight, touch and smell, a conjunction of sense associations which Dickens uses elsewhere in this childhood section: the 'memorable birthday', for instance, when news of his mother's death comes:

> How well I recollect the kind of day it was! I smell the fog that hung about the place; I see the hoar frost, ghostly, through it; I feel my rimy hair fall clammy on my cheek; I look along the dim perspective of the schoolroom . . . (9: 175)

In chapter 2, the perceptions are more specifically childish: the exaggerating vision of 'Peggotty, with . . . eyes so dark that they seemed to darken their whole neighbourhood in her face', the toddler's perspective upon the fowls 'that look terribly tall to me', the splendid evocativeness of 'the touch of Peggotty's forefinger . . . roughened by needlework, like a pocket nutmeg-grater', and the first of the many smells in the novel—that of the 'mouldy air' wafting out of the

[1] 'Dickens: the Two Scrooges', in his *The Wound and the Bow* (revised edn, London 1952), 38–9.

storeroom 'in which there is the smell of soap, pickles, pepper, candles, and coffee, all in one whiff' (61–2). Smells have a special potency in David's memory:[2] the smells of Salem House, of the crape and cakes at his mother's funeral, of the sea air mixed with the perfume of flowers which means sanctuary at Dover ('As I laid down my pen, a moment since, to think of it, the air . . . came blowing in again, and I saw [the whole interior] . . . and my dusty self upon the sofa, taking note of everything' (13: 250)), the 'earthly smell' and 'sunless air' of Canterbury Cathedral which are still 'wings that take me back . . .' (18: 322), the scent of a geranium leaf, always associated with a special day in his courting of Dora (its scent, 'at this day, strikes me with a half comical, half serious wonder as to what change has come over me in a moment' (26: 456)), the smell of Clara Peggotty's beefsteak pie, 'curiously flavoured' by the miscellaneous odours ascending from the shop over which her brother was lodging ('I recollect [it] well' (32: 533)).

Immediately, too, in 'I Observe', Dickens establishes his command of the logic of children's thinking: David's fear of the dark store-room at night, his worries after hearing about Lazarus, his fresh-eyed scrutiny of the monumental tablet to Mr Bodgers in the village church ('I wonder whether they called in Mr Chillip, and he was in vain; and if so, how he likes to be reminded of it once a week' (2: 64)). These early chapters abound in such felicities, sometimes supplemented, for narrative convenience, by afterthoughts ('for my later understanding comes, I am sensible, to my aid here' (2: 67)) and sometimes with a subtler technique which allows the adult reader to perceive meanings which the witnessing David could not discern ('I could observe in little pieces, as it were; but as to making a net of a number of these pieces, and catching anybody in it, that was, as yet, beyond me' [2: 70]). As has often been remarked, the attractiveness of this novel is due, considerably, to the fact that, as Forster put it, 'it can hardly have had a reader, man or lad, who did not discover that he was something of a Copperfield himself' (Life, 555). George Orwell happily caught this aspect of the earlier chapters, when he

---

[2] Unsurprisingly, David shares this characteristic with Dickens. In the essay on 'Dullborough Town' in The Uncommercial Traveller, Dickens remarks on the momentous childhood coach-journey which took him from Chatham to London, that 'Through all the years that have since passed have I ever lost the smell of the damp straw in which I was packed?' This is very close to David's reminiscence of his equivalent journey to London: 'the smell of stables (ever since associated with that morning)' (5: 123). Of one of the smells mentioned below, it may be noted that the geranium was Dickens's favourite flower.

recalled first reading the book, as a boy, and vaguely imagining that it had been written by a child. David is, in this respect, a more representative boy than the child in Wordsworth's *Prelude*—who, for instance, is never (in retrospect) funny, and the emotional range of whose experience is narrower, more specialized. Admittedly, David's is, in Edmund Wilson's phrase, 'an idealized version' of childhood. Partly, of course, the idealization is deliberate (on Dickens's part), the product of the child's magnifying vision still cherished in the enchanted memory: and this very common feeling about one's childhood is gently recognized for what it is by the adult David—the fruit clusters on the trees outside his birthplace, for instance, were 'riper and richer than fruit has ever been since, in any other garden' (2: 65). But a more limiting idealization is that David—according to his own account, and we are not (I think) invited to query it at this point—is never naughty (he surely has the reader's sympathy when he bites his tormentor Murdstone), never contrary or bad-tempered or selfish or moody. Perhaps he was too close here to his virtuous creator to be representative: for the Dickens family servant Mary Weller recalled young Charles as being 'not quarrelsome as most children are at times.' In this regard, the Tulliver children in *The Mill on the Floss* are more typical; David is spared some of the less agreeable characteristics of children by having no brothers or sisters to quarrel with, but Pip in *Great Expectations*, another lone orphan, exhibits more human imperfection than David. Pip of course has the disadvantage of being born ungenteel but wanting to be a gentleman, as Emily in *David Copperfield* yearns to be a lady—ambitions which expose them to temptation. Pip, however understandably, becomes a snob; David, in the Murdstone and Grinby episode, might be called one, but unlike Pip he does not suggest that any such self-reproaches might be appropriate.

But, though some notes are not sounded, Dickens never strikes a wrong note in this part of the book. The re-creation of childhood joys is unfailingly felicitious. Better perhaps than trying to recollect my own childhood for purposes of comparison, I look at my children, and think how they too would delight in and treasure the memory of Peggotty's 'work-box with a sliding lid, with a view of St Paul's Cathedral (with a pink dome) painted on the top' (2: 65), and would share David's enchanted view of the picture over Mr Peggotty's mantelshelf—a picture of the Sarah Jane lugger, . . . with a real little wooden stern stuck on to it; a work of art, combining composition with carpentry, which I considered to be one of the most enviable possessions that the world could afford' (3: 79); how evidently, for them, a prospect which is 'very satisfactory' is 'therefore not at all improbable' (3: 85); how they on the eve of a holiday feel an excitement like David's ('I would have given any money to have been allowed to wrap myself up over-night, and sleep in my hat and boots' (2: 76)), and how, when happy, they exist in an eternal present like David and Emily: 'The days sported by us, as if Time had not grown up himself yet, but were a child too, and always at play. . . . We made no more provision for growing older, than we did for growing younger' (3: 87). Only Shakespeare, in English literature, I think, has as finely caught this sense of being

> lads that thought there was no more behind
> But such a day tomorrow as today,
> And to be boy eternal   (*A Winter's Tale*, I.ii.63–5)

and the imagery of Dickens's phrases does not suffer in the comparison. And such generalizing re-creations of the moods of childhood ('as if Time had not grown up himself yet . . .') are amply backed up by Dickens's imaginative command of the specific, sometimes, as in the following quotation, presented in such a way as to provoke questions about the nature of mind and memory:

I don't know why one slight set of impressions should be more particularly associated with a place than another, though I believe this obtains with most people, in reference especially to the associations of their childhood.[3] I never hear the name, or read the name, of Yarmouth, but I am reminded of a certain Sunday morning on the beach, the bells ringing for church, little Em'ly leaning on my shoulder, Ham lazily dropping stones into the water, and the sun, away at sea, just breaking through the heavy mist, and showing us the ships, like their own shadows. (3: 91)

But of course not all the childhood experiences which haunt David's memory and affect his development are of this idyllic quality. To start from his most obvious deprivation: he never saw his father, his mother (though charming and lovable in some aspects) lets him down badly, his

---

[3] A notion, and phrase, which meant much to Dickens: he originally published two of his *Uncommercial Traveller* essays, 'Dullborough Town' and 'Nurse's Stories', under the title 'Associations of Childhood'. Another essay relevant to this theme is 'New Year's Day' (*Household Words*, 1 January 1859, reprinted in *Miscellaneous Papers*).

stepfather is a bully, hateful and hating him, and then his mother dies when he is ten, and he has no brothers or sisters and only one remote and eccentric relative—though Betsey Trotwood proves a wise and generous supporter when at last he seeks her out. It is noticeable how many of the characters of David's generation—almost all of them, indeed—come from similarly sparse families. This is a situation that Dickens was fond of, but none of his novels has so many under-parented and un-siblinged children. Orphans include David, Emily, Ham, Traddles, Jack Maldon, Rosa Dartle and Martha Endell. Others of that generation have one parent—Steerforth, Uriah, Agnes, Dora, Julia and Annie—but, as several of them remark, they receive wrong or inadequate guidance from him or her. 'I was very young, and had no adviser. Between mama and me, in all relating to you,' Annie tells her husband, 'there was a wide division' (45: 731). Steerforth wishes to God that he had 'had a judicious father these last twenty years!' (22: 380). Of all the young people in the novel, only Sophy Crewler has any brothers or sisters: she has two parents, too, but this is not allowed to be to her advantage.

Dickens of course was not the only novelist to be attracted towards the orphan or poorly-parented young hero or heroine, whose situation is both pathetic and fraught with challenges which the less lonely child is spared. Thus, to revert to two partly-autobiographical novels already mentioned, Jane Eyre, like David, is alone in the world (whereas Charlotte Brontë, like Dickens, came from a good-sized family, though she had indeed lost her mother), and George Eliot gives Maggie Tulliver just one brother (she herself came from a family of five) and parents who, through their stupidity, create difficulties for Maggie more severe than her creator had experienced. David, it may be added, suffers a greater shock and anguish in the Murdstone and Grinby episode than any of the childhood tribulations of Jane or Maggie. That episode is closely based on what happened to Dickens at the age of twelve, as was noted above; it is indeed fascinating to compare chapter 11 with Dickens's autobiographical fragment (it may be found in Forster's *Life*, bk. I, chs. 1 and 2), for exactly half of its text is copied, with slight verbal revisions, from that manuscript, with the newly-imagined episodes interspersed, and of course the matters relating to Dickens's parents (financial difficulties, imprisonment, etc.) attributed to David's new acquaintances, the Micawbers. No less striking, as an instance of the novel's 'blending of imagination and experience', is the equal vividness and reality of the following chapters, depicting David's flight from London to Dover,

which all seem to be Dickens's creation; certainly his own release from
Warren's Blacking warehouse came in no such way. These chapters
present another interesting contrast. During the warehouse episode,
partly because it is more static, we hear much more about David's
feelings (though note again the mixture—this account of 'the secret
agony of my soul' is kept from becoming morbid by the interspersed
comic scenes introducing the Micawbers), but the presentation of
David's flight to Dover, having more action and movement, is less
concerned with his reactions, though his terror, weariness and hope are
quite sufficiently conveyed. The people he meets on this journey provide
a good example of Dickens's vivification of character, even in such one-
time encounters: the long-legged young man who makes off with
David's box and half-guinea, Mr Dolloby who buys the waistcoat, old
Charley (the 'goroo' man), and the tinker who seizes the handkerchief,
are all strongly individualized. Dickens visualizes places, too, very
sharply: David certainly speaks for him when he remarks 'I looked at
nothing, that I know of, but I saw everything' (27: 463):

> At last I found a shop that I thought looked promising, at the corner
> of a dirty lane, ending in an inclosure full of stinging nettles, against the
> palings of which some second-hand sailors' clothes, that seemed to
> have overflowed the shop, were fluttering among some cots, and rusty
> guns, and oilskin hats, and certain trays full of so many old rusty keys of
> so many sizes that they seemed various enough to open all the doors in
> the world.
>
> Into this shop, which was low and small, and which was darkened
> rather than lighted by a little window overhung with clothes, and was
> descended into by some steps, I went with a palpitating heart; which
> was not relieved when an ugly old man, with the lower part of his face
> all covered with a stubby, gray beard, rushed out of a dirty den behind
> it, and seized me by the hair of my head. He was a dreadful old man to
> look at, in a filthy flannel waistcoat, and smelling terribly of rum. His
> bedstead, covered with a tumbled and ragged piece of patchwork, was
> in the den he had come from, where another little window showed a
> prospect of more stinging nettles, and a lame donkey.
>
> 'Oh, what do you want?' grinned this old man, in a fierce,
> monotonous whine. 'Oh, my eyes and limbs, what do you want? Oh,
> my lungs and liver, what do you want? Oh, goroo, goroo!'

                                                            (13: 239–40)

(As a contrast in literary method, look at chapter 28 of *Jane Eyre*, presenting Jane's flight from Thornfield: she meets half a dozen people, but they remain anonymous and indistinct.)

'His offence, and confinement upstairs,' runs Dickens's note for chapter 4. '*Child's remembrance of the latter.*' For chapter 9, he notes: 'Mrs Creakle breaks it to him. His state of mind—childish incidental whimsicalities.' The childish perspective and reactions are finely caught—the five days' confinement which 'occupy the place of years in my remembrance', the feeling of being important because his mother had died which 'was a kind of satisfaction to me' (4: 109, 9: 177)—though sometimes another way of regarding the experience is suggested, often by the tone of the narratorial voice: the light irony, for instance, of the description of David's dismay when Mr Dolloby prices the waistcoat ('"I should rob my family," he said, "if I was to offer ninepence"')—'This was a disagreeable way of putting the business; because it imposed upon me, a perfect stranger, the unpleasantness of asking Mr Dolloby to rob his family on my account' (13: 236). Often too of course the reader sees that David is misunderstanding, or not fully comprehending, an episode, though Dickens is very sparing in making this point explicitly, as he is sparing too in making 'little did I then know . . .' hints about how the plots will develop. A good example of both these points is the Salem House encounters with Steerforth—his taking care of David's money ('I hastened to comply with his friendly suggestion'), his yawning enquiry about whether David has a sister ('I should have liked to know her'), and his 'very noble' treatment of Mr Mell (6: 137, 140, 7: 154). David's hero-worship of Steerforth—very credible, particularly in a lonely boy who has never had a father or other older man to look up to—is his first major error of judgment. Like his other such mistake—marrying Dora—it springs from an amiable weakness (over-estimating people is a more pleasing fault than its opposite), and the childhood chapters show how circumstances, and heredity, encourage him to develop this 'romantic and dreamy' tendency. He is an only child, and a lonely one; Blunderstone seems singularly devoid of children for him to play with,[4]

[4] To be sure, a genteel boy living in a village with few genteel families could then be very lonely. But Dickens is no good at villages. He has no feeling for the community life of a village, the social structure, the way a country boy would spend his time, etc.; Pip's village, in *Great Expectations*, is as vague as David's, and even less populated. As in other respects, George Eliot complements Dickens here; each can do, effortlessly, many things which lie outside, or close to the edge of, the other's range.

as later he does not want to become intimate with Mick Walker or Mealy Potatoes, and, apart from the holiday idylls with Emily, Steerforth and Traddles are the first friends he makes.

Dickens draws attention to this weakness in David, with a hint that it will have bad consequences (though, in retrospect, we may also relate it to David's later becoming a successful novelist): 'Whatever I had within me that was romantic and dreamy, was encouraged by so much story-telling in the dark; and in that respect the pursuit may not have been very profitable to me' (7: 146). There are unmistakable narratorial warnings, too, that both Emily and Steerforth are to come to no good. She is evidently destined for a fate worse than death: after she has seemed close to drowning, David reflects, 'There has been a time since . . . when I have asked myself the question, would it have been better for little Em'ly to have had the waters close above her head that morning . . .' (3: 86), and as this episode follows her confession that 'I should like so much to be a lady' it is easy to guess how she will fall. Easy to guess, too, with whom: for just after the glamorous Steerforth has asked David whether he has a sister, David falls to sleep dreaming about him, and the chapter (and No. 2) ends with a dark hint: 'No veiled future dimly glanced upon him in the moonbeams. There was no shadowy picture of his footsteps, in the garden that I dreamed of walking in all night' (6: 140). As Steerforth is later to exclaim, 'You romantic Daisy!' (20: 349): and it is noticeable that David is in a particularly 'romantic' and susceptible mood at two crucial moments in his early adult life—he is dazzled by his visit to the theatre, when he runs into Steerforth again (19: 344), and, just before he first meets Dora and 'falls into captivity' (an ominous phrase in retrospect), he has been feeling very 'alone in the world, and much given to record that circumstance in fragments of English versification' and is now so 'enchanted' by Mr Spenlow's 'lovely garden' that, before even meeting Dora, he thinks 'What a beautiful name!' (26: 446, 450)

An important feature in which the child David is father of the man is the similarity between Dora, whom he loves to distraction at first sight, and his beloved mother. (This is all the more evident when one re-reads the novel.) Clara Copperfield describes herself as 'but a childish widow' (1: 53), Dora echoes this with 'but a child-wife' (44: 711). Both have pretty faces and hair and good figures; both are delicate, and die young. They are impractical and domestically incompetent, they are treated as children by other adults and are dominated by their servants. They are silly, wilful and pettish, though both are of fundamentally sweet and loving disposition; when crossed or criticized, they go off into self-pitying irrelevancies about their having lately done some loving deed, Clara forgoing a parasol because the money was needed for David, and Dora walking miles and miles to buy her husband a salmon (2: 69, 44: 704). Clara on such occasions, however, tends to be more peevish and infantile than Dora—though, indeed, Dora is never humiliated and maltreated as badly as Clara. Still, Dora might have repeated some of Clara's reproaches to her husband: 'I thought you were pleased, once, with my being a little inexperienced and girlish, Edward—I am sure you said so—but you seem to hate me for it now, you are so severe' (4: 100). Clara's being pushed harder, and being more babyish, is illustrated by a comparison between these two speeches: when Murdstone tells her that his feeling for her is 'chilled and altered' she implores him, 'very piteously, "Oh, don't, Edward! I can't bear to hear it. Whatever I am, I am affectionate. I know I am affectionate. I wouldn't say it, if I wasn't sure that I am. Ask Peggotty. I am sure she'll tell you I'm affectionate"' (4: 100). Dora is pitiable, too, when she begs David to call her his 'child-wife', but she does not have to grovel so low for love: 'When you miss what I should like to be, and I think can never be, say, "still my foolish child-wife loves me!" For indeed I do!' (44: 711)—and David's response, of course, is much warmer than Murdstone's. (This was the point at which, effectively and affectingly, Dickens ended the David/Dora part of his *Copperfield* public reading.)

Men often seek, unconsciously, for a bride who resembles their mother. David is the more prone to do this because he is an only son and only child, who inevitably becomes specially fond of his mother: and there is no father for him to love or with whom he must share his mother's affection. Predictably David is worried about her ever remarrying (this is the subject of his first conversation in the book), and he is immediately jealous and resentful of Murdstone before he has had any chance to discover how oppressive and hateful this new man in his mother's life really is. (It is not surprising that Sigmund Freud particularly admired this novel.) Dickens presents this situation with great insight: and the chapter in which David discovers that he has 'got a new Pa' ends splendidly—it is the conclusion of Number 1, too—with David's finding much else altered, and wandering disconsolately into the yard and encountering that terribly proleptic dog:

I very soon started back there, for the empty dog-kennel was filled up with a great dog—deep-mouthed and black-haired like Him—and he was very angry at the sight of me, and sprang out to get at me. (3: 93)

One other point which Dickens is making about David's pre-disposition to love a girl who resembles his mother is that he is very much the son of the father he never saw. This is hinted at by their having the same name: and how essential this was to Dickens's conception of the character appears in the fact that, in the many titles for the novel which he tried out in his notes, the hero—whether he was named David or Thomas or Charles, Copperfield or Mag—was always, except in three out of seventeen instances, specifically 'the Younger' or 'Junior'.[5] Mr Chillip tells David that 'There's a strong resemblance between you and your poor father, sir' (60: 904), and Mr Dick (that wise fool) keeps calling him 'David's son'. He first does so a page after Betsey Trotwood has mentioned one of his father's proclivities in which he will indeed 'strongly resemble' him: for David senior, too, 'was always running after wax dolls from his cradle' (13: 252–3). On a later occasion when Mr Dick reverts to this likeness (and he is much like his mother, too, Betsey says), a note of warning follows: '"But what I want you to be, Trot," resumed my aunt, ". . . is a firm fellow. With resolution. . . . That's what your father and mother might both have been, Heaven knows, and been the better for it"' (19: 332). A few pages later, however, he experiences what he 'always considered . . . as the first fall I had in life'—his being so easily and ignominiously ousted on the coach—and he connects this to 'a distrust of myself, which has often beset me in life on small occasions, when it would have been better away' (19: 342): and it is made clear how whatever tendencies of this kind may plausibly be attributed to heredity

[5] When Mr Barkis discovers that Peggotty's Christian name is Clara, 'He seemed to find an immense fund of reflection in this circumstance' (8: 161). So should we, since she shares this name with David's mother. The names of many other characters are worth reflecting about: Murdstone's and Steerforth's are obvious examples (Betsey makes explicit part of the significance of the former when she calls him 'Murderer' (13: 253)). Also, as many commentators have remarked (e.g. Sylvère Monod, *Dickens the Novelist* (Norman, Oklahoma 1968), 301–3), the nicknames, pet-names or new names which characters give one another tell us much about both namer and named. For instance, reflect upon who calls David (and why?) Brooks, Davy, Mas'r Davy, Master Copperfield, Daisy, Young Innocence, Trotwood, Trot, Mr Copperfull, and Doady. Dora's actually asking to be called 'child-wife' has been noted; Betsey—a constant re-namer—calls her Little One, Little Blossom, etc., diminutives which Dora's behaviour justifies, indeed.

were fostered by the insecurities of his childhood. Two pages further on, he runs into Steerforth, who conspicuously possesses and effortlessly uses just the qualities which David lacks and envies at this stage: self-confidence, *savoir-faire*, a nonchalant charming command of any situation.[6] Again one sees why David 'blindly' admires Steerforth: and again Dickens emphasizes how Steerforth, the man with whom David is most intensely involved and who manifestly (as I have remarked) is more his moral and emotional complement than his 'bad angel',[7] is, like him, a victim of heredity and of nurture. Not only do they both lack 'a judicious father' (22: 380) but also Steerforth, like David, much takes after one of his parents, different though the two lads' parentage is (32: 531–2). Rosa Dartle, a percipient though not a dispassionate witness, later inveighs against Mrs Steerforth about her son's 'inheritance of your nature', and bids her 'moan and groan for what you made him! . . . Moan for your nurture of him, moan for your corruption of him. . . !' (56: 871). The Murdstones bully David's mother, but they lack the finesse and the foreknowledge of the adult David's mistakes which would give them the chance to reproach and distress her in these terms, as they might well have done. Rosa's accusation sets up, nevertheless, one of the echoes which sound across a novel so full of young people growing up in unpromising circumstances.

[6] The adverb most associated with Steerforth is *easily*: e.g., '. . . his head reclining *easily* on his arm . . .' (6: 140; cf. 29: 498 and 55: 866, all passages at the ends of the chapters named). *Lightness* is another Steerforth word: thus he charms the Barkises to 'a kind of *adoration* for him'—as earlier he had cast 'a *spell*' upon Mr Peggotty and Ham, by 'an *ease* in his manner—a gay and *light* manner it was, but not swaggering—which I *still* believe to have borne a kind of *enchantment* with it' (7: 157)—because 'in everything [he did there was] an indescribable *lightness*, a seeming impossibility of doing anything else, or doing anything better, that was so graceful, so *natural* and agreeable, that it overcomes me, *even now*, in remembrance' (21: 368). My italics throughout. The *still* and *even now* continue the sequence of hints that Steerforth is dangerous in ways that David had not realized. He is a victim to the *spell* or *enchantment*, but not the only one, which helps to excuse him, though the despised or patronized Traddles is sensibly immune to it.
[7] See above, p. 22.

3. The Adult David

This, we have seen, is the first Dickens novel in which the hero is presented fully both as child and adult: and I have mentioned G. K. Chesterton as one proponent of a judgment often made, that his success is incomplete. Chesterton wrote, in his Introduction (1907) to the Everyman *David Copperfield*:

> In the amazing earlier chapters . . . , he does seem to be going to tell the living truth about a living boy and man. It is melancholy to see that sudden fire fading . . . to see David Copperfield turning into Nicholas Nickleby. Nicholas Nickleby does not exist at all; he is a quite colourless primary condition of the story. . . . But David Copperfield does begin by existing; it is only gradually that he gives up that rather exhausting habit.

Chesterton attributed the alleged failure to the novel's autobiographical origins: Dickens had begun with the intention of telling the whole truth about himself, but had 'gradually allowed the whole truth to be more and more diluted.' Certainly any autobiographical novelist experiences particular disadvantages and temptations, as well as unique advantages. In some senses, he is writing on his best-known and best-loved topic, himself; but we are all blind to important aspects of ourselves. The autobiographical novelist may feel also unable to tell the whole living truth, both out of consideration for the feelings of intimates who appear recognizably in his novel, and from delicacy about reporting his own merits and successes or an inability to face the pain or shame of his failures and shortcomings. And, beyond all such emotional and prudential considerations, such an author must of course be novelist first and autobiographer second: fiction is a different art form from autobiography, and 'life' cannot go into 'art' unaltered.[1]

One failure in the presentation of the adult David does more credit to Dickens's modesty and circumspection than, here, to his artistry: the hero's emergence as a successful and prosperous novelist. For Dickens to have made David succeed at his own unprecedently spectacular level would have hamstrung him at far too many other points: the David/Dickens assimilation would have been, for the readers he had to think about (he didn't need to bother about us), embarrassingly complete. So David is credited instead with enough professional competence for his life to be a success story. But on what it feels like to be a novelist and a celebrity, David is conspicuously—indeed, deliberately—silent: 'I do not enter on the aspirations, the delights, anxieties, and triumphs of my art. That I truly devoted myself to it with my strongest earnestness, and bestowed upon it every energy of my soul, I have already said. If the books I have written be of any worth, they will supply the rest' (61: 917). He had said much the same in his one other reference to his art: his fictions 'express themselves, and I leave them to themselves' (48: 758). Now this is a reasonable thing for an actual novelist to say, and Dickens often said it (for example, prefacing his 1847 Cheap Edition: 'It is not for an author to describe his own books. If they cannot speak for themselves, he is likely to do little service by speaking for them'). But it is an absurdly unhelpful thing for an *imaginary* novelist to be made to say, for we cannot turn to the *Works of David Copperfield*. It was a mistake for Dickens to make his hero a novelist if, for whatever

---

[1] The relations between David and his creator, and some of the problems of autobiographical fiction, have been fully discussed by, among others, Sylvère Monod (see Select Bibliography), Philip Collins (in *Essays and Studies*, 1970) and Angus Easson (in *Literature and History*, 1975). Studies of the real-life originals of other characters include K. J. Fielding's of Micawber and Miss Mowcher (*Listener*, 19 July 1951), Margaret Cardwell's of Rosa Dartle, William Oddie's of Micawber and P. F. Skottowe's of Traddles (*Dickensian*, 1960, 1967 and 1969), and Philip Collins's of Creakle, as teacher and magistrate (*Dickens and Education*, 1963, and *Notes and Queries*, 1961). The origins of particular episodes and scenes have been discussed by K. J. Fielding ('*David Copperfield* and Dialect', *Times Literary Supplement*, 30 April 1949), W. J. Carlton ('An Echo of the *Copperfield* Days' and 'The "Deed" in *David Copperfield*', *Dickensian*, 1949 and 1952), and Philip Collins ('*David Copperfield* and East Anglia', *Dickensian*, 1965). Literary influences on the novel have been surveyed by Earle Davis in his *The Flint and the Flame: the Artistry of Dickens* (London 1963) and Harry Stone in 'Fairy Tales and Ogres: Dickens's Imagination and *David Copperfield*' (*Criticism*, 1964).

reasons, he felt so reluctant to flesh out the assertion that David succeeded in this line—for a creative writer's work is likely to be much more intimately connected with his life and personality than, say, an engineer's or banker's or parliamentary reporter's. Dickens plays false here to the art he professed, for he well knew how much self-commitment beyond 'my strongest earnestness' goes into creation: and if 'every energy of my soul' was exerted, such an effort obviously deserved more detailed attention in a novel purporting to be about its hero's 'Personal History and Experience'. David need not be reticent about discussing his creative work: Dickens's refusal to 'describe his own books' in a printed preface, from delicacy, pride and a sense of propriety, is irrelevant in a book ostensibly written 'for no eyes but mine' (42: 671). David indeed makes that remark to excuse his patting himself on the back for working so hard to master 'that tremendous shorthand'—a process to which he devotes, disproportionately, far more space than to describing his eventual career as a famous novelist. The emptiness of this phase of David's adult experience results, surely, from an unsatisfactory balance between Dickens and his hero: and Dickens does too little to make David's turning to authorship seem probable, let alone inevitable. On rereading the novel, one pays more attention to a few scattered phrases in the earlier chapters: he was 'a child of excellent abilities, and with strong powers of observation' who had 'hopes of growing up to be a learned and distinguished man' (11: 208, 210)—not that, when he returns to school, he is seen to be actively in pursuit of learning, though he responds vividly to Fielding and Smollett, and retells the stories to Steerforth and friends. He is certainly an imaginative boy. But nothing further is heard of any pleasure in reading or writing, until suddenly in chapter 43 he has taken to authorship, and by chapter 46 he is beginning to be famous. Too many crucial developments are happening offstage here. This is not a matter of criticizing David for not being Dickens (an error into which it is easy to fall), or not a novelist in his likeness: rather it is to say that his existence as a novelist is so perfunctory as to be nominal. Thackeray in *Pendennis* also concentrates on his hero's personal life, but when Pen emerges through journalism into authorship a modicum of attention is spared to indicate how a budding author might credibly get started upon his career, and what some of 'the aspirations, the delights, anxieties, and triumphs' of writing mean to the practitioner.

Still, as I have remarked, this novel is much less concerned with the public world, and the job world, than most of Dickens's. A pointer is given by David's first speech—with which may be compared the child Paul Dombey's first speech in the preceding novel: 'Papa, what's money? . . I mean, Papa, what can it do?' (*Dombey and Son*, ch. 8). This refers emphatically enough to its novel's dominant theme. David, like-wise interrogatory, has another preoccupation, which is also his novel's:

> 'Peggotty,' says I, suddenly, 'were you ever married? . . . You mustn't marry more than one person at a time, may you, Peggotty? . . . But if you marry a person, and the person dies, why then you may marry another person, mayn't you, Peggotty?' (2: 65–6)

Like much else in these early chapters, this, as has been indicated, means more on a rereading: intelligible enough as the worried boy's concern about the intruder Murdstone, this dialogue also carries the rereader ahead to David's marrying a person who dies, and then marrying another person. More simply, the hero's first words suggest that marriage is to be a preoccupation of this novel.

Fiction, like stage comedy, has traditionally been much concerned with courtship, the usual finale being a loving tableau or wedding bells or hints about progeny. As Byron complained in 1821,

> Romances paint at full length people's wooings,
> But only give a bust of marriages;
> For no-one cares for matrimonial cooings. . . .
>
> (*Don Juan* III, viii)

The notion that matrimony is much a matter of cooings is Byron's sardonic joke; Dickens has his David put it more delicately and more realistically. The last stages of his engagement to Dora, and their wedding, are presented entirely as 'a dream' ('Nothing is real') and the honeymoon begins with Dora's skittish but chilling question, 'Are you happy now, you foolish boy? and sure you don't repent?' (43: 695, 700; end of No. 14). The first—and ensuing—chapter about the married David, entitled significantly 'Our Housekeeping', begins with the light irony of David after the honeymoon finding himself 'quite thrown out of employment, as I may say, in respect of the delicious old occupation of making love,' and then trying to adjust himself to the queer fact that

> there we were, alone together as a matter of course—nobody's business any more—all the romance of our engagement put away upon a shelf, to rust—no one to please but one another—one another to please, for life . . .

—that final phrase a brilliant brief throwaway summary of what, splendidly and dauntingly, it means to be married. Within a page occurs the first dialogue we hear in the marital home: 'our first little quarrel' (44: 701–2). Dinner is an hour overdue, and David has work to do: he is learning the hard way about the inadequacy of his notions of love and marriage and 'romance'.

For, if Dora is, as David tells her during that first quarrel, 'very childish, and . . . talking nonsense', he has been childish too. His state of mind after becoming engaged to her was hardly more mature than when he rambled hand in hand with Emily, in a dream of 'never growing older, never growing wiser, children ever' (10: 202). David indeed makes the point, at the beginning of his courtship: 'As to marriage, and fortune, and all that [a nicely give-away phrase!], I believe I was almost as innocently undesigning [too kind an adjective] then, as when I loved little Em'ly' (26: 454; interjections mine). Thus, after becoming engaged:

> I suppose we had some notion that this was to end in marriage. . . . But, in our youthful ecstasy, I don't think that we really looked before us or behind us; or had any aspirations beyond the ignorant present. . . .
>
> What an idle time! What an insubstantial, happy, foolish time! Of all the times of mine that Time has in his grip, there is none that in one retrospect I can smile at half so much, and think of half so tenderly.
>
> (33: 551)

'Foolish', but 'happy': and the terms 'smile at' and 'tenderly' characterize the handling of this courtship and marriage. What could have been presented as a terrible warning, or an agonizing or at least vexatious experience, is made predominantly an occasion for delightful comedy, with tender and pathetic moments and a little grave reflection. This is partly because, with all her shortcomings, Dora is genuinely warm and often charming, and David, though disappointed, is remarkably patient (he never loses his temper with Dora, at her most feckless and exasperating) and remains affectionate. Dickens remits the darker possibilities of love gone sour and awry to other areas of the novel, notably Steerforth and Rosa Dartle. Moreover, David's follies and tribulations are those traditional in young lovers—the absurdities of courtship (apparent to the perpetrators, afterwards), the minor disasters of newly-weds (ghastly meals, tiffs, and so on). David often refers to the typicality of his follies and weaknesses: over the picnic for Dora's birthday, for instance, 'I committed two small fooleries which other young gentlemen in my circumstances might have committed—because they came so very natural to me' (33: 542). As he says elsewhere, 'What is natural in me, is natural in many other men, I infer' (32: 516), and he refers to 'the contradictions and inconsistencies . . . within me, as there are within so many of us' (39: 361). Most interestingly, David is uncertain how typical is his fate when he is forced to acknowledge to himself that his marriage is unsatisfactory:

> The old unhappy feeling pervaded my life. . . . I loved my wife dearly, and I was happy; but . . . there was always something wanting. . . . What I missed, I still regarded—I always regarded—as something that . . . was incapable of realization; that I was now discovering to be so, with some natural pain, as all men did. But that it would have been better for me if my wife could have helped me more . . . ; and that this might have been; I knew.
>
> Between these two irreconcilable conclusions: the one, that what I felt was general and unavoidable; the other, that it was particular to me, and might have been different: I balanced curiously, with no distinct sense of their opposition to each other. (48: 765)

This inability to hold in consciousness, let alone resolve, a painful contradiction is indeed a good instance of the self-protective evasions that 'there are within so many of us'.

As Forster (quoted above, p. 28) suggests, David's thus playing Everyman is an important part of the novel's appeal and character. He has lately been seen as a more specifically representative figure, however, in Dr Q. D. Leavis's impressive reassessment of the novel, which includes the most substantial recent defence of it against such criticisms as Chesterton's, Dickens was here examining, she says, 'the experience of growing up in the first half of the 19th century, with the problems that a young man of that generation incurred.' She praises 'Dickens's strikingly intelligent apprehension of the need for both romantic tenderness and devoted services to sustain the male ego in its struggle with the conditions of living in such a world as the Dickens world, in a competitive society; and the impossibility of combining these qualities in a single personality.' Her argument commands respect, but I cannot accept it, nor her conclusions. David's belonging to the 1830s–40s has its importance, but this is a much less time-bound book than the spate of novels, around this time, about the problems faced by young men of that generation:

Disraeli's *Coningsby* (1844) and *Tancred* (1847), for instance, or Newman's *Loss and Gain* (1848), Kingsley's *Yeast* (1848) or Clough's verse-stories *The Bothie* (1848) and *Amours de Voyage* (written in 1849). Nor am I convinced by Mrs Leavis's 'impossibility . . .' (though it's a lucky man, in any period, who finds a wife who possesses every desirable quality; the novel, it should be added, is much less concerned with what qualities a wife may hope to find in her husband): and, by the time David marries, he is not in fact having to 'struggle . . .' (he is doing very well), though he would prefer to have his meals on time and to have a wife who could make a more vital contribution to his career as an author than holding his pens. And Dr Leavis's argument entails her seeing David as 'colourless and intentionally uninteresting in himself'—a backhanded defence, surely, since a minimal qualification for the hero of a novel, if he is to command attention, is that he be interesting. I find David so, though I think that Dickens failed to extract all the moral and psychological interest inherent in the situation.[2]

I have mentioned above (pp. 20, 25) Dickens's making David postpone his account of 'the state of my mind beneath its load of sorrow', and have suggested that the necessity of keeping the other plots in play is one reason why Dickens does not press hard enough to explore his hero's mind at some crucial moments. Perhaps too, in a first-person novel, David's being so nice-minded (and often so dense, so slow to see what ought to be obvious) is a disadvantage: in the quotation from chapter 48, just above, for instance, the statement that 'I was happy' is inadequately related to 'the old unhappy feeling' of two sentences before. That chapter, 'Domestic', is the climax of the Dora story: David's last hopes that she will grow up, and his attempts to 'form her mind', collapse; he recognizes, to some extent, his disappointment; at last he realizes why Annie Strong's phrases about the 'undisciplined heart' and 'unsuitability of mind and purpose' have been haunting him: he resolves to accept Dora for what she is, 'and still be happy'—and then 'Dora was not strong' and the chapter ends with the clear intimation that she will release him from his mistake by dying soon. Here, and in chapter 58, 'Absence', are the most extended probings of David's adult mind (including its 'secret feelings'): and, despite many felicities, I find them disappointing—partly because, as David says, 'I cannot so completely penetrate the mystery of my own heart, as to know' important particulars about it (58: 889). Dora, by

[2] The passages quoted are in F. R. Leavis and Q. D. Leavis, *Dickens the Novelist* (London 1971), pp. 46–9, but Mrs Leavis's argument should be studied in full.

contrast, never disappoints: she is thoroughly imagined, both in her scatty charm and in her pathos, and Dickens is skilful in giving us enough access to her mind for the novel's purposes—her recognition here, for instance, that the marriage is a mistake, and that David should have married Agnes ('Are you sure you don't think, sometimes, it would have been better to have—' (48: 764), a speech which David typically fails to understand). And, a few lines later, her babyish expression is just right: David tells her that he loves her as she is, and—'"Without a story—really?" inquired Dora, creeping closer to me.' But when, five chapters later, she dies, telling David on her deathbed that this is a good thing ('It is better as it is. . . . It is much better as it is' (53: 837–8)) one sees the inadequacy and vagueness of the presentation of David: 'As I look out on the night, my tears fall fast, and my undisciplined heart is chastened heavily—heavily' (53: 838). It should have been devastated, or, if it was not, we should have been made to realize and reflect upon the fact: for he should be appalled to have brought his young wife to the point where she sees it as 'much better' for her to die than to live. But as Ross H. Dabney remarks, this episode is 'all quite unreal'; Dickens is not intending us to see David as psychologically guilty of Dora's death, nor to wonder whether there is any kinship between him and Murdstone, the 'murderer' of Dora's twin-figure Clara: 'Dickens is merely ashamed of doing away with Dora for his hero's convenience and is trying to make it nicer by having her show understanding and willingness to go along'. Clara's death had been an occasion for real sorrow, but Dora's is 'something to be got over, with appropriate gestures, as quickly as possible.'[3]

Dickens never presses hard enough on David, in these reaches of the book. As the news that 'Dora was not strong' comes too pat, within a page of his acknowledging his folly in having married her, and as her deathbed scene and his subsequent alleged grief are muffed, so too 'what [my heart] had felt in its secret experience' (48: 766) is examined too cursorily and too gently. David makes more fuss, here and elsewhere, about the revelations he is to make of the 'secrets' of his heart than, when revealed, they seem worth. At an earlier stage of his disillusionment, for instance, in the chapter on 'Our Housekeeping' and just after Dora has opted to remain his 'Child-wife', he relates how he kept his 'many anxieties' (about his work, too, it seems) to himself: 'I am far from sure,

[3] Ross H. Dabney, *Love and Property in the Novels of Dickens* (London 1967), 71–3.

now, that it was right to do this, but I did it for my child-wife's sake' (a promising line of thought, this, but David does not further explain or pursue it). He continues:

> I search my breast, and I commit its secrets, if I know them, without reservation to this paper. The old unhappy loss or want of something had, I am conscious, some place in my heart; but not to the embitterment of my life. . . . I did miss something of the realization of my dreams; but I thought it was a softened glory of the Past, which nothing could have thrown upon the present time. I did feel . . . [etc.]; but. . . . (44: 713)

This has some felicity in its notation of a reluctant half-recognition of disappointment and failure, and of an unhappiness by no means absolute: and it has behind it the phrase, reiterated half-a-dozen times in the novel, which appropriately had, at its first introduction, instead of the adjective 'old', 'a *vague* unhappy loss or want of something' (35: 565, just after David has first discussed with Betsey Trotwood his engagement to Dora, and she has indicated, to the reader more fully than to him, her sense that he is marrying the wrong girl—'blind, blind, blind!'). But 'softened'—an adjective used in the passage from chapter 44 quoted above—describes the impact of this 'secret experience' of David's breast; or—to revert to the difficulties of first-person narration—David is too kindly to express the anguish of his situation, and Dickens lacks the skill at this stage (he had acquired it by the time he made Pip narrate *Great Expectations*) to indicate to the reader a subtext complementing or contradicting what the hero says. What results is an undisturbing account of an unfortunate marriage: no recriminations, no despair, but exemplary generosity on both sides, with Dora dying willingly and offstage, and selflessly bequeathing her husband to 'the real heroine' ('she made a last request to me,' Agnes recalls after David, a widower and now unblinded, finds her conveniently still unmarried and proposes to her, 'and left me a last charge, . . . that only I would occupy this vacant place' (62: 939)). It is all too pat.

What it feels like to be caught up in a misalliance appears more honestly in *Middlemarch* (1872) where, eminently in the fiction of this period, George Eliot finds the veracity and the imagery for the predicament which David Copperfield and Tertius Lydgate face, as rising young professional men married to uncomprehending flibbertigibbet wives with, as their pathetic claim to a rational existence, some command of the 'accomplishments' so overvalued at this period and so widely criticized by novelists, educational reformers and feminists. Lydgate like David is slow and reluctant to acknowledge the gravity of his mistake. 'What I am describing,' writes David after giving his 'secret' thoughts, 'slumbered, and half awoke, and slept again, in the innermost recesses of my mind. There was no evidence of it in me; I know of no influence it had in anything I said or did' (48: 766)—and certainly we see no evidence of its having any influence. This is how George Eliot describes Lydgate at a similar point:

> He was intensely miserable, this strong man of nine-and-twenty and of many gifts. He was not saying angrily within himself that he had made a profound mistake; but the mistake was at work in him like a recognised chronic disease, mingling its uneasy importunities with every prospect, and enfeebling every thought. (ch. 58)

And the strongly physical imagery ('chronic disease') recurs at a later stage of Lydgate's disillusionment:

> The first great disappointment had been borne: the tender devotedness and docile adoration of the ideal wife must be renounced, and life must be taken up on a lower stage of expectation, as it is by men who have lost their limbs. (ch. 64)

Granted the many differences between David and Lydgate, and their wives, the force and honesty of George Eliot's writing in passages such as these indicates why I cannot regard the corresponding parts of *David Copperfield* as major fiction, such as *Middlemarch* undoubtedly is.[4]

The narrative of David's life with Dora succeeds at a light-comic, not at a serious or potentially tragic, level. The Everyman follies and

[4] I revert to the *Middlemarch* comparison below (p. 53): both novels also contain a young woman married to a middle-aged or elderly ineffectual scholar, who has some reason to suspect that his wife is attracted to a younger man. As I have suggested elsewhere (*Times Literary Supplement*, 18 May 1973), *Middlemarch* may have been a conscious reworking of some *Copperfield* materials; certainly comparisons between the two novels are instructive. Many readers of the serialized *Middlemarch* were waiting for Rosamond to emulate Dora by dying and thus allowing Lydgate to marry more happily: but George Eliot left him sweating it out (though she did release Dorothea from her misalliance, by Dr Casaubon's sudden death). George Eliot, it may be added, knows what being a scholar means: Casaubon's futile project is entirely plausible, whereas Dickens has no more than a *Punch*-joke apprehension of Dr Strong's alleged Dictionary of Greek Roots.

extravagancies of courtship, the comicality of David's proposing while 'Jip barked madly all the time' during his most impassioned pleadings (33: 549), the tiffs and troubles of their prolonged engagement, with her delectable Aunts as enthusiastic referees at one stage, and then the not-too-terrible annoyances and disappointments of their 'Young Housekeeping'—all these are presented much more fully and effectively than David's analysis of what, emotionally, the marriage meant to himself (or to her). At least, however, the Dora story is both touching and diverting. Dickens achieves less when he tries, in the Agnes story, to be more serious over marriage. This is partly because Agnes has nothing to do except wait around, good and patient and wise, until David proposes and she can confess that 'I have loved you all my life!' (62: 937)—a speech which, interestingly, Dickens had orginally planned to give to David (Number-plan XIX–XX). At her first introduction, nearly all her attributes are mentioned, and they are repeated at most subsequent re-entries—a method which works, as has been remarked, for such comic characters as Micawber, but which becomes tediously over-insistent with a straight character. 'Then come and see my little housekeeper,' says Mr Wickfield, and there she is with her keys and her adjectives—*placid*, *sweet*, *tranquil*, *bright*, *happy*, *quiet*, *good*, *calm*, *grave*—and with her religiose associations ('a stained glass window in a church' [15: 279–80]). These and other such paraphernalia often recur in profusion: inside one page, for instance (35: 572–3), *love and truth* appears three times, accompanied by *mild*, *gentle*, *bright*, *good*, *radiant*; or, inside another (39: 631–2), *peace* and *rest* and *sister* appear twice, with, inevitably, *placid*, *tender*, *sweet*, *beaming*, *Heavenly* and *sacred*.

Unlike Dora, she is not visualized: Dora has that delightful 'shape' and pretty hair, Agnes merely has sides against which her keys hang, and the adjectives about her all refer to her disposition and moral qualities. And, unlike Dora, she (and David's feelings about her) cannot be laughed at. 'I don't think I had any definite idea where Dora came from, or in what degree she was related to a higher order of beings,' David writes; 'but . . . I should have scouted the notion of her being simply human, like any other young lady, with indignation and contempt' (33: 535). Earlier, he had 'made a very angel' of little Em'ly (3: 87). No such irony is directed against David's perpetually seeing Agnes in terms of the sacred or angelic, nor are we invited to notice a discrepancy here, nor to question the wisdom of his categorizing her in this way; instead, the novel ends, emphatically, with her 'face, shining on me like a Heavenly light' and a final invocation to her as 'my soul' and the hope that, when he dies, he will 'still find thee near me, pointing upward!' Nor, as I remark later, does Dickens invite us to feel troubled about the 'sisterly' aspect of this relationship. 'I love little Em'ly, and I don't love Agnes—no, not at all in that way—but I feel that there are goodness, peace, and truth, wherever Agnes is' (16: 289): but, when he marries Agnes, is there any sign that he has come to love her at least somewhat 'in that way'? Rather, does not the repeated 'sister' reference continue to make her an asexual if fondly cherished being, a tendency reinforced by the religious references ('You are always my good angel . . . I never think of you in any other light' (35: 376)?

Many excellent qualities are imputed to Agnes, but she is not interestingly dramatized. Her inexorably unruffled sweetness of disposition becomes incredible when, for instance, David inquires whether the school-teaching to which she has been driven by her father's misfortunes is not laborious, and she replies: 'The labour is so pleasant that it is scarcely grateful in me to call it by that name' (60: 913). This is a silly thing to say (there is a truer ring about Charlotte Brontë's remark 'that none but those who had been in the position of a governess could ever realize the dark side of "respectable" human nature'), but Dickens does not intend it to be seen that way. Given that union with Agnes is the divine event towards which this whole creative achievement moves, one sees why Angus Wilson (for instance), who enormously admires the 'memory' aspect of David Copperfield ('quite the artistic equal of A la Recherche du temps perdu') becomes exasperated at the end and sees 'this most inner of Dickens's novel' as also his 'most complacent—indeed, in the pejorative sense of that word, the most Victorian', partly because of the 'philistine, bourgeois, complacent views of his [Dickens's] powers as a writer' reflected by David (views which Agnes firmly encourages), and also, among other things, because the apprehension of love, in the David story, falls so far short of an intelligent inquiry into the meanings of love and passion. 'He has mocked at romantic love,' Angus Wilson continues, 'at the distorting power of passion; yet the complacent domestic fireside of Agnes seems an empty thing to put in its place'[5]—a thing which should, one might add, be overshadowed by the memory of the silly but sweet and dead Dora, who loved him ('For indeed I do!') and whom he had loved as he never purports to love Agnes.

Angus Wilson's description of the novel as Dickens's 'most Victorian'

[5] Angus Wilson, The World of Charles Dickens (London 1970), 214–16.

provides, perhaps, a second-best line of defence for this part of it: for the novel appears in a significant list compiled by the *doyen* of Victorian studies, G. M. Young:

> The books which, taken together, seem to me to give the truest idea of family life, its standards and morals, in the Victorian age, are the first volume of [Ruskin's] *Praeterita*, *David Copperfield*, Mrs Ewing's *Six to Sixteen*, the (anonymous) *Book with Seven Seals*, and Mrs. Hughes's *London Child of the Seventies*.[6]

Only a few years after *Copperfield*, a vastly popular narrative poem on marital love began to appear, Coventry Patmore's *The Angel in the House* (1854–62)—and no novelistic heroine combined the Angelic with the Housekeeper more insistently than Agnes. Nor can it be altogether coincidental that in Thackeray's semi-autobiographical novel *Pendennis*, serialized alongside Dickens's, the hero marries his 'sister' Laura—though neither author had in fact married a young woman with whom he had been brought up and thus induced to regard in an affectionate but asexual way. To marry a wholesome, competent, sisterly young woman with (to revert to the Agnes/Dora comparison) sides but no form or face or enchanting manner, evidently represented salvation from the time-honoured clash between Love and marital and social Duty, here presented in muted middle-class form. As George Orwell neatly put it, Agnes is 'the real legless angel of Victorian romance, almost as bad as Thackeray's Laura'[7]—but neither David nor Dickens seems to notice or bother about her deficiencies or her lover's complaisance in overlooking them. To revert to an earlier comparison, Dickens is later more intelligent about Pip's love-life, though Biddy and Estella are, indeed, no more a repetition of Agnes and Dora than David is a pattern for Pip. And again Charlotte Brontë provides a complement to Dickens. One of the girls in her *Shirley* (1849) protests that

> 'If men could see us as we really are, they would be a little amazed; but the cleverest, and acutest men are often under an illusion about women; . . . they misapprehend them, both for good and evil: their

---

[6] G. M. Young, *Victorian England: Portrait of an Age* (London 1936), p. 153 n.

[7] Orwell, *Critical Essays* (London 1946), p. 54. There is an excellent discussion about why intelligent men like Dickens and Thackeray felt so enthusiastic over this decidedly limited feminine ideal in Alexander Welsh's *The City of Dickens* (London 1971).

good woman is a queer thing, half doll, half angel; their bad woman almost always a fiend. . . .' (ch. 20)

and she continues with criticisms of heroines in fiction. In *Copperfield*, the doll-angel is split into Dora and Agnes, with Rosa as the fiend—but, as will be suggested, she is an interesting little devil.

4. *David as Observer and Participant*

As I remarked, much of the novel consists of plot developments in which David is more observer than participant: and this is particularly so after he has become an adult and is a less intensely interested observer than in his childhood when everything affected him personally ('How strange it seems, and new!'). Most of these developments are indeed thematically related to the David story, in that they concern love and marriage. Even the Uriah Heep plot, which is fired mostly by his envy and cupidity—the humble worm turning into vengeful serpent—has its sexual aspect too, since he wants to get Agnes as well as her father's firm, and thus arouses David's instinctive jealousy (the fine episode at the end of chapter 25, for instance). The Micawbers, too, relate to this theme, not only because Mrs Micawber 'will never desert Mr Micawber' but also because theirs is the most perfect marriage in the book, the most enjoyable both for the happy couple and for the reader. But, splendid creations as they are, the Micawbers' contribution to the novel much exceeds their relevance to the marriage theme, and I shall return to them.

The other non-David parts of the novel are a mixed bag, and some (it must be admitted) are poorly done. That mysterious man haunting Betsey Trotwood, for instance: this action was not worth embarking upon if Dickens was to do so little with it. It explains of course why Aunt Betsey was so set upon David's being a girl, but such an explanatory action is best kept off-stage (as Dickens does when explaining Miss Havisham's similar reasons for hating men, in *Great Expectations*). This mysterious man in the shadows—a conventional figure in much fiction of this time—does not occupy much time or attention, however, so he does no great damage to the novel. The Annie Strong story is a greater weakness. It is there mainly to throw up the phrases used by Annie in the *éclaircissement* scene, which strike David 'as if they had some particular interest, or some strange application that I could not divine' (he is incredibly obtuse, sometimes)—'There can be no disparity in marriage like unsuitability of mind and purpose', 'the first mistaken impulse of my undisciplined heart', 'my love was founded on a rock, and it endures!' (45: 729–32) But too little is done with Annie to make her protestations as convincing and moving as they should be. Here the first-person method of narration increases Dickens's difficulties: we have too little access to Annie's mind until the *éclaircissement*, when she has to speak almost non-stop for six pages. But also Dickens is quite unwilling to explore, in depth, the formidable emotional, physical and practical problems inevitable in the marriage of so young a woman to so elderly a man: instead, a haze of love and gratitude arises to romanticize what, in default of an honest confrontation of these problems, must seem a nauseating or at best a most abnormal and unpromising marriage. Inevitably one contrasts George Eliot's treatment of this May-and-December situation in *Middlemarch*, where another ineffective scholar marries a bride much his junior. Dorothea and Dr Casaubon are of course much more prominent characters than Annie and her husband, but it is not only the amount but also the quality of attention, the emotional honesty and the intellectual command, which make George Eliot's achievement here act as a devastating critique of the flimsy evasiveness of this part of *David Copperfield*.

A similar 'infection of claptrap'—Dickens's phrase, on another occasion—affects the Emily story, though again the presentation of Emily, as of Annie, suffers from our having inadequate (because it is exterior) access to her mind and motives. There are some effective glimpses—her wanting to be a lady, her scene with Ham at the end of chapter 22—but her most articulate moments (her long letters to her uncle) ring false in sentiment and expression, much though they hit the taste of the time. Thackeray regarded Emily's letter (which one is not specified) as emphatically 'a masterpiece', and Dickens's rendering of the chapter 31 letter, in his Public Reading, was found very moving; he was highly gratified by its effect on a Parisian audience which had struck him as particularly sophisticated—'a low murmur of irrepressible emotion went about like a sort of sea' (*N* III, 340). He was proud of what he had achieved with this character in the novel, feeling, he said, 'a great hope that I shall be remembered by little Em'ly, a good many years to come' (*N* II, 201); he also hoped 'to do some good' by encouraging a more charitable attitude to such 'poor girls' (*N* II, 94), about whom indeed he knew a lot, for he was then superintending a home for fallen women in Shepherd's Bush.

Emily's situation was a stock one in Victorian drama and fiction—the lower-class girl with a faithful lover of her own class, and an unscrupulous well-to-do admirer who plays upon her desire to be, or to enjoy the trappings of, a lady. The girl is usually either ruined and disgraced (e.g. Hetty Sorel in Eliot's *Adam Bede*) or eventually returns repentant to her faithful lover (e.g. Mary Barton in Mrs Gaskell's novel). In *David Copperfield*, Dickens's treatment of the situation does not rise much above the conventional; his work at Shepherd's Bush was far more realistic and intelligent. He accepts, for instance, the cliché judgment that seduction is a fate worse than death (3: 86, quoted above, p. 32). Emily is never allowed to enjoy one moment of her fallen life and, when rescued and exported, she is not allowed to marry, though she has many offers. Here, as over Annie Strong and Martha Endell, Dickens is disabled, partly by his extraordinary regard for the sexual propriety and reticence of his age; he is, indeed, more mealy-mouthed than Mrs Gaskell and George Eliot, who state or suggest more of the facts of such matters and never become as airy-fairy as he does in his account of Dora's pregnancy and miscarriage (48: 766–7) or as absurdly theatrical as he makes his Martha appear in her 'Oh! the river!' speech (47: 749). Martha never sounds like a Norfolk girl turned London whore, but like an actress playing a very corny role, with over twenty blank-verse lines in that chapter alone. Blank verse (always a bad sign in Dickens) invades Mr Peggotty, Agnes and Rosa, too, at climactic moments.

The Emily part of the book is not wholly unsuccessful, however. The Yarmouth scenes are marred by some class-condescension on Dickens's part, but he always achieves some felicities in presenting such cosy domestic episodes, which were highly regarded by his original readers. In Mrs Gummidge he tosses off one of those summaries of human behaviour which have achieved the status of a proverb. Her 'I feel it more' and 'everythink goes contrary with me', like the Spenlow and Jorkins notion, are smaller examples of Dickens's fertility in creating the proverbial, of which Micawber's expectation that 'something will turn up' is the great type. The Micawber phrase, and the attitudes behind it, represent such a recurrent situation in life—what Chancellor of the Exchequer since 1849 has *not* appeared as Micawber in political cartoons?—that it seems remiss of earlier English authors not to have invented it, and an inexcusable deprivation for earlier generations to have had to do without it. Being sure that 'I feel it more', like waiting hopefully for something to turn up or (as Oliver Twist does) wanting some more—these are among the most obvious of human fates and proclivities: and it is one of Dickens's supreme gifts that he feels the obvious with such force and plenitude that he can encapsulate it in the proverbial phrase or situation. Not that his range is restricted to the 'obvious'; he has an equally sharp sense of the improbable and extraordinary.

To return to the Yarmouth group: Dr Q. D. Leavis finds the presentation of Mr Peggotty remarkable, in ways that earlier critics have not suggested:

> ... while Mr Peggotty seems at first sight to offer the pattern of disinterested devotion to the winning child he had fostered, what emerges is a horribly possessive love that is expressed characteristically in heat, violence and fantasies, impressing us as maniacal. And Dickens doesn't attempt to disguise this; on the contrary, it is hammered home.
> (*Dickens the Novelist*, 79–80)

She makes out an interesting case, but I do not find (I wish that I could) that this meaning consistently underlies the ostensibly noble, loving and forgiving uncle (and that is certainly how Dickens presented Peggotty in his Public Reading). Nor do I think that Dickens was disturbed by what may indeed be regarded as something morbid in this relationship between uncle and niece, any more than he was by other confusions in the novel between familial and sexual roles—Annie's 'Oh, my husband and father' attitude to Dr Strong (45: 724), for instance, or David's 'Agnes! Sister! Dearest!' at his proposal (62: 934). It would have been a more interesting novel, in these areas, had he been disturbed by these confusions: and if Mrs Leavis is right, Mr Peggotty is certainly much more interesting than I find him.[1] There are limits (often quite surprising

---

[1] A novel which Dickens might have written, had he added other strengths to those which he possessed and had he been more aware of his weaknesses, has been indicated in Robert Graves's revised and abbreviated version, *The Real David Copperfield* (London 1933). 'Dickens's honesty failed him' Graves maintains, particularly on sex, class and religion; also he was tempted to waffle, to fill those twenty long Numbers. Apart from two major inventions—a passionate reunion between Emily and David, who confesses that class differences prevented his acknowledging his love for her, and her subsequent suicide—Graves's alterations are mostly deletions, and small twists in how events are presented. E.g., after Annie's declaration to her husband: 'I was glad for him [David remarks] . . . that

ones) to Dickens's understanding and wisdom, particularly in sexual matters. David took after him in being 'blind, blind, blind' here. Thus, I am surprised by Dickens's letters of 1855 to the original of Dora (Maria Beadnell, now Mrs Maria Winter) when she accidentally and tragi-comically re-entered his life: she was soon thūs to re-appear in his fiction, devastatingly, as Flora Finching, the ludicrous but pathetic old flame of the hero of *Little Dorrit*. But, at the time, Dickens told her that he hoped she had recognized 'touches of your old self' in Dora—and he did so with no suggestion that to find oneself depicted as Dora might be other than an agreeable and flattering experience.

The major success on the Emily side of the novel are Steerforth and his group (Mrs Steerforth, Rosa Dartle, Littimer, and Miss Mowcher). Rosa is a most original and perceptive creation. Perhaps because he is less intent upon preserving our sympathy for her (as he is for Emily and Annie and the other girls in difficult sexual situations), Dickens probes more fully into the distortions of personality, the anguish and violence and resentment, which result from her impassioned relationship with the Steerforths: 'I concluded in my own mind that she was about thirty years of age, and that she wished to be married. She was a little dilapidated—like a house—with having been too long to let [here Dickens permits David to make too easy a joke for this context]; yet had . . . an appearance of good looks. Her thinness seemed to be the effect of some wasting fire within her which found a vent in her gaunt eyes' (20: 350). Rosa is almost always convincing, and startling, both in her quieter moments of sly needling ('Are they, though? . . . I want to know *so* much') and in more violent passages such as the harp episode (29: 495–7) and her later scenes with Mrs Steerforth. Only in her scene with Emily does Dickens lose control, and Rosa's speech becomes false and strained ('reserve your false arts for your dupes . . . , you purchased slave' (50: 787)). Another figure in the Steerforth group begins well: at her first

---

Annie had chosen to say what she had, even if it was untrue' (she eventually marries Jack Maldon). Or in the finale: 'As was inevitable, I eventually married Agnes. . . . On the whole, I have been very happy . . . though on my side there are no strong romantic feelings; perhaps marriage is better without them. . . . Everything in the house has its proper place, the meals are well-cooked and regular. . . .' In an Appendix, chapter 62 is reprinted 'as a reminder of the sort of writing' which Graves has spared the reader. This is an amusing, and sometimes shrewd and suggestive, *jeu d'esprit*. W. Somerset Maugham, too, made an abridged version of *Copperfield* (London 1948): but I have not examined it.

appearance, Miss Mowcher is a brilliantly original grotesque, but then the actual dwarf who lived round the corner from Dickens, and upon whose physical peculiarities he had unkindly drawn, wrote to protest, so he had, in recompense, to make her a 'good' character, implausible though this is after her first appearance, when it is clear that among 'the variety of ways' in which she made herself useful (22: 395) was by acting as a procuress. Her protestation to David that she had believed that 'it was *you* [not Steerforth] who had a boyish passion' for Emily (32: 524) is entirely unconvincing, if one re-reads the scene: but it was the best that Dickens could do to restore his neighbour's reputation and peace of mind.

Steerforth himself is a much more interesting figure than the 'villain' in fiction of this period generally becomes. I have discussed his charm, and Dickens does more than assert it: he convincingly shows it at work, and not only upon David. As we have only limited access to his mind, and we never see him after the first half of the book, much about him remains a mystery: and David, it may be remarked, hardly ever says anything penetrating about his character—or about other characters. For a novelist, David is surprisingly incurious about other people's minds. But analysis was not Dickens's usual way, either, of presenting and exploring character. What was his usual way is illustrated by a moment which Mrs Leavis neatly picks on, Steerforth's remark about Traddles: '"Oh! That fellow!" said Steerforth, beating a lump of coal on the top of the fire, with the poker. "Is he as soft as ever?"' (28: 486). As she remarks, it is not only Steerforth's attitude to the amiable Traddles, but his accompanying action of beating the lump of coal (and it is David's fire, not his), that convey to us 'without having to analyse or intellectualize it, the selfish and arrogant and even cruel streaks in Steerforth, such as his ready contempt for others, that point to his subsequent brutal treatment of Emily. We see Dickens evolving this habit of making symbolic actions convey character-traits yet which are so natural that we hardly notice the symbolism' (*Dickens the Novelist*, 101). Sometimes we do have direct glimpses of the complexities which lie beneath the charm and the egoism—his self-hatred, his nihilism, his anxiety to be loved by David even while he patronizes him—notably in the 'reproachful ghost' episode at Yarmouth when he is a 'torment' to himself (22: 379), his 'Ride on!' philosophy (28: 487), and his 'I wish, I wish, I wish, you could give [the nickname "Daisy"] to me!' (29: 497). I have referred to his being a foil and complement to David; and maybe he too derives from Dickens, reflecting aspects of him which did not go into David—his dynamism, his darker and less estimable moods and qualities.[2] It is regrettable that the novel's form, and its other preoccupations, prevented Steerforth's character being further developed and explored. Dickens evidently well understand, and was fascinated by him: it is notable that he gives him such a splendid death—Ham's dying receives much less attention—waving his red cap in the storm which drowns them both and which is presented with such remarkable force. It was, for Victorian critics, the standard example of Dickens's command of the sublime, as his platform performance of that episode, during which he wept over Steerforth's death, was by general consent the grandest moment in all his public readings. Attuned to the critical *convenances* of a century later, readers may now be more impressed by the evidence that the manner of Steerforth's death is elaborately foreshadowed by the imagery (e.g. 46: 742).

The most remarkable creation in the Copperfield world is obviously, however, Mr Micawber; his legendary status has already been mentioned. Notoriously, he is the product of observation and memory as well as of Dickens's imagination, for much of Micawber's grandiloquent idiom, as well as some of his misfortunes, derive directly from Dickens's father. Thus, when John Dickens was moving house, his creditors tried to catch him before he flitted: as he put it, 'My preparatory demonstrations of migration have led to what may be called a vote of "want of confidence", which tends much to the embarrassment of my financial arrangements.'[3] Happily, Micawber too uses 'migration' as his word for moving house (36: 593, 597). Elsewhere, explaining that he is not able to pay a debt on time, John Dickens writes, 'I am looking forward with some hope'—which anticipates Micawber's most famous tag-phrase. Other such likenesses abound: but Dickens seems to have invented the characteristic 'in short' with which Micawber deflated his own grandiloquence—a fine finishing touch. Mrs Micawber, however, bears little relation to Dickens's mother, but was created as the

[2] See for example Pamela Hansford Johnson, 'The Betrayal of Self in Literature', *Listener*, 3 March 1949, 367–8. Interestingly, Steerforth's 'Ride on!' imagery and idea are repeated by Dickens in letters about his anguish and restlessness shortly before the break-up of his marriage—'Too late to say, put the curb on,' 'die in harness,' 'one is driven by an irresistible might until the journey is worked out!' In another letter of this period (1855–8) he compares himself to 'poor David' with his sense of 'one happiness I have missed in life' (*Life* 638–9).

[3] Quoted in K. J. Fielding's article in *The Listener*, 19 July 1951.

ideal helpmeet and foil for her husband—the novel's perfect example of marital 'suitability of mind and purpose'. They both inhabit the same dream-world, which helps. Mrs Micawber thinks otherwise, indeed, and makes a distinction which is clearer to her than the reader: 'I have not the sanguine disposition of Mr Micawber. My disposition is, if I may say so, eminently practical' (57: 880). She may say so, but she is in such accord with him as to talk, as blithely and with as little regard to actuality as he, of 'the great probability of something turning up' (17: 319). When speaking 'with her most affable air of business' it is to proclaim her fantasy of her husband, newly appointed a clerk to Wickfield and Heep, becoming a Judge or Chancellor (36: 596). She performs her role perfectly, too, in the emotional volatility which has become the family way of life—threat of suicide one moment, ordering hot kidney pudding and a plate of shrimps the next—never deflating her husband with common sense or a reminder of facts, but unfailingly rising to his every mood, with an evident enjoyment of the drama which matches his: as David observes, 'Mrs Micawber was just the same' as her spouse in this respect (11: 219). Reading over the marriage service 'with a flat-candle' on the eve of her wedding (28: 593)—and what a superbly irrelevant vivifying touch that flat-candle is!—may have added a meritorious sense of duty done to Emma's fidelity to her Wilkins, but an emotional and intellectual harmony so complete as theirs needs the sanctions of neither religion or law to protect it. The only threat to it is the prosperity and tranquillity of Australia; can they, we object, be happy without their accustomed diet of disaster?

Micawber is of course strongly visualized—and we see him, inevitably, not only through Dickens's words but also in the shape given to him by 'Phiz'. (Dickens's novels are, with some of Thackeray's, the only adult fiction in English the original illustrations of which have become an integral part of the text.) The exterior manifestly proclaims the man. Body-shape and costume, mannerism and gesture, are all emblematic of his character. Thus, at his first appearance:

> His clothes were shabby, but he had an imposing shirt-collar on. He carried a janty sort of a stick, with a large pair of rusty tassels to it; and a quizzing-glass hung outside his coat,—for ornament, I afterwards found, as he very seldom looked through it, and couldn't see anything when he did. (11: 210)

This, with his 'large and very shining' head and 'very extensive' face, catches his nature—genial, jovial, expansive, pretentious (imposing/shabby, jaunty/rusty) but with hope, or pretence, triumphing over the threatened disgrace or disaster. And, as was noted (above, p. 18), he is always 'all complete': at every appearance he repeats his act, Dickens being wonderfully fertile in gratifying expectation without letting the act become stale or mechanical. Micawber delights in his own nature and in the act he has created:

> 'I have no scruple in saying . . . that I am a man who has, for some years, contended against the pressure of pecuniary difficulties.' I knew he was certain to say something of this kind; he always would be so boastful about his difficulties. (17: 316)

> '. . . It may reasonably be inferred that our baby will first expire from inanition, as being the frailest member of our circle; and that our twins will follow next in order. So be it! For myself, . . . imprisonment. . . .' Much affected, but still intensely enjoying himself. . . . (52: 825–6)

For of course we *hear* Micawber as well as see him. Like the other great Dickens characters—Mrs Gamp and Mr Pecksniff, for instance—he is a great rhetorical performer. All of them luxuriate in words; they hold forth at great length, in their own highly distinctive idiom; they are all very literary, both in being fond of allusion (Biblical or poetical) and in creating their own kind of splendid bad poetry—'The canker is in the flower. The cup is bitter to the brim. The worm is at work, and will soon dispose of his victim. The sooner the better. But I will not digress' (49: 770).

Micawber's activity in the Heep plot, I have suggested, is unsatisfactory. As George Orwell put it, referring to 'the needless ramifications of Dickens's novels, the awful Victorian "plot"': 'In the end even people like Squeers and Micawber get sucked into the machinery. . . . They start off as magic-lantern slides and they end by getting mixed up in a third-rate movie.' Micawber, indeed, is less important to the narrative of the novel than to its overall meaning: and, extravagant and eccentric though he may seem, he encapsulates a truth about humanity beyond Dickens's constant useful reminder that 'there *are* such people [as his "caricatures"]; we are such people ourselves in our true moments, in our veritable impulses; but we are careful to stifle and hide those moments from ourselves and from the world', as George Santayana put it, adding that 'When people say Dickens exaggerates, it

seems to me they can have no eyes or ears.' I conclude by citing two
critics (and fellow-novelists) who had imperfect sympathies for Dickens
and his fiction but who warmed to Micawber and to the novel which he
inhabits: Henry James, regarding 'the fantastic' as Dickens's great
resource, saw Micawber as one of 'the exaggerated statements of types
that really existed. We had, perhaps, never known a . . . Pecksniff, nor a
Micawber; but we had known persons of whom these figures were but
the strictly logical consummation'—such as Chancellors of the
Exchequer. The other imperfect sympathizer is Virginia Woolf who, in
an essay on this novel, finely acknowledges how Dickens 'has the
visualizing power in the extreme' ('As a creator his peculiarity is that he
creates wherever his eyes rest'—as they don't, we have noticed, upon
Agnes), but then she sharply calls into question the integrity of his
method: 'With such a power at his command Dickens made his books
blaze up, not by tightening the plot or sharpening the wit, but by
throwing another handful of people upon the fire.' Such fecundity, she
implies, is enviable but irresponsible; his novels tend to become bunches
of 'separate characters loosely held together, often by the most arbi-
trary conventions.' But in *Copperfield*, she acknowledges, what
characters!—'As we listen to Micawber pouring himself forth and
venturing perpetually some new flight of astonishing imagination, we
see, unknown to Mr Micawber, into the depths of his soul.' And he
contributes notably to the overall effect of this novel which, she says,
surmounts the danger of these vivid characters' flying asunder and
splitting the reader's attention:

> There [in *Copperfield*], though characters swarm and life flows into
> every nook and cranny, some common feeling—youth, gaiety,
> hope—envelops the tumult, brings the scattered parts together, and
> invests the most perfect of all of the Dickens novels with an atmosphere
> of beauty.[4]

---

[4] George Orwell, *Critical Essays*; George Santayana, *Soliloquies in England*
(London 1922); Henry James, *Nation*, 21 December 1865; Virginia Woolf, *The
Moment and other Essays* (1947); all reprinted in Wall (see Bibliography), 302, 311,
265, 165, 275–6.

Select Bibliography

The standard biography is Edgar Johnson's *Charles Dickens: his Tragedy and Triumph* (2 vols, London 1953), but John Forster's *Life of Charles Dickens* (1872–4, often reprinted) remains invaluable, and it contains the fragmentary autobiography which parallels chapter 11, and other parts, of *Copperfield*. The definitive *Pilgrim* edition of the *Letters* (ed. Madeline House *et al.*, London (1965–) is replacing the *Nonesuch* edition (ed. Walter Dexter, 3 vols. London 1938). The text of Dickens's *Copperfield* reading, with particulars of how he performed it, is in the *Public Readings* (ed. Philip Collins, London 1975). The items asterisked in the 'General Works' listed below have particularly helpful chapters on *Copperfield*. Most of these have been reprinted in paperback.

General Works

G. K. Chesterton, *Charles Dickens* (London 1906)

Humphry House, *The Dickens World* (London 1941)

*Sylvère Monod, *Dickens romancier* (Paris, 1953; revised and translated as *Dickens the Novelist* (Norman, Oklahoma 1967))

George H. Ford, *Dickens and his Readers* (London 1955)

*John Butt and Kathleen Tillotson, *Dickens at Work* (London 1957)

*J. Hillis Miller, *Charles Dickens: the World of his Novels* (London 1958)

K. J. Fielding, *Charles Dickens: a Critical Introduction* (London 1958; revised 1965)

*Philip Collins, *Dickens and Education* (London 1963)

—— (ed.), *Dickens: the Critical Heritage* (London 1971: reception of his works, 1836–82)

*Angus Wilson, *The World of Charles Dickens* (London 1970)

Stephen Wall (ed.), *Charles Dickens* (Penguin Critical Anthologies, 1970)
*F. R. and Q. D. Leavis, *Dickens the Novelist* (London 1971)

Studies of David Copperfield

Virginia Woolf, 'David Copperfield' (1925: in her *The Moment and Other Essays*, London 1947; reprinted in Wall, above)

Robert Graves, *The Real David Copperfield* (London 1933): criticism by a revised and abbreviated version.

Gwendolen B. Needham, 'The Undisciplined Heart of David Copperfield', *Nineteenth Century Fiction* IX (1954), 81–107

Ross H. Dabney, *Love and Property in the Novels of Dickens* (London 1967), ch. 2

Vereen M. Bell, 'The Emotional Matrix of *David Copperfield*', *Studies in English Literature* (Texas) VIII (1968), 633–49

Roy Harvey Pearce (ed.), *Experience in the Novel* (New York 1968): essays by J. Hillis Miller and K. J. Fielding

George J. Worth, 'The control of emotional response in *David Copperfield*', in *The English Novel in the Nineteenth Century*, ed. George Goodin (Urbana, Illinois 1972)

Robin Gilmour, 'Memory in *David Copperfield*', *Dickensian* LXXXI (1975), 30–42

Michael Black, 'David Copperfield: self, childhood and growth', in his *The Literature of Fidelity* (London 1975)

(Essays on the autobiographical origins of *Copperfield* are listed in footnote 1 to chapter 3 (p. 39).)

Index